Nadia's babies w[...] received a phone call from Saudi Arabia informing her that her babies and her mother-in-law had crossed the border safely. She breathed a huge sigh of relief.

Nadia and her husband, Mansoor, were leaders in the Kuwaiti resistance movement since Iraqi troops invaded Kuwait. They had no illusions about the severity of the punishment if they were discovered. Feeling incumbered regarding the safety of their little ones, they made the painful decision to send the children across the border into Saudi Arabia. They knew the trip through the desert would be an enormous risk, but they felt that occupied Kuwait would become more violent as the days passed.

Nadia felt her heart would break as she watched her children being driven away. Her emotions ranged from great hope to darkest terror. The long hours that she knew her babies were in acute danger were the hardest of her life. Any mother would understand the agony. But now she knew she had made the correct choice. Her babies were safe.

•

The Rape of Kuwait

•

THE
RAPE
OF
KUWAIT

The True Story of
Iraqi Atrocities
Against a
Civilian Population

Knightsbridge Publishing Company
New York

Published in the United States by
Knightsbridge Publishing Company
255 East 49th Street, Suite 25D
New York, NY 10017

ISBN 1-56129-193-5

Designed by Laura A. Janetzke

10 9 8 7 6 5 4 3 2 1
First Edition

To all the innocent people of all nationalities who lost their lives during the invasion of Kuwait.

And, especially, to Sheik Fahd Ahmed Al-Jabir Al-Sabah, who was killed the first day of the invasion by Iraqi soldiers while defending the home of his brother, the Emir of Kuwait.

Ah! Woe is me!
Would that I had never
Taken such a one
For a friend!

Koran: SXXV.28—Mohammed

Contents

•

Acknowledgments

The birth of any book is difficult. This particular work was especially wrenching due to the painful subject matter and the scarcity of time.

Regardless of my determination to tell the tragic stories of yet another group of innocent individuals caught in a war not of their making, this book would have never been completed without the assistance of many people. There are those who I cannot name due to their very real fears for the safety of their loved ones. They know who they are and I silently acknowledge each of them. I take special pleasure in recognizing those whose names I can mention in this acknowledgment.

I am forever indebted to the Kuwaiti ambassador to Washington, Sheik Saud Nasir Al-Sabah, who was invaluable in helping me to establish contacts. Dr. Hassan A. Al-Ebraheem and Dr. Samir Hawana graciously took the time to assist me. Ali Al-Abdalla Al-Sabah, counselor at the embassy, went out of his way to make me feel comfortable in requesting assistance. Joy Rivera, whose warmth and quickness in retrieving needed material never faltered, deserves a special thank you.

In Cairo, Dr. Balkees Al-Najjar was my source of strength and proved to be of inestimable value. To the Kuwaiti ambassador to Egypt, Abdulrazzak Al-Kendari, my deep appreciation.

In Riyadh, the entire staff of the Kuwaiti embassy were tireless in their endeavors to assist me in any manner possible: Suliaman Al-Shakeen, Ahmed, Lafi, Sami, Abdullah, Ferial, and my driver, Sadeen. Ahmed's sense of humor surfaced at difficult moments and he will never be forgotten.

A mere thank you to Mr. Suliaman Mutawa, the minister of planning of the Kuwaiti government, is inadequate in view of his unwavering support.

Without Dr. Souad Al-Sabah and her son Mohammed, I might not have made the last few steps.

Of course, there were many others who supplied moral support simply because they are friends. Nancy Apple, Peter Sasson, and Julie Lawson Sasson were always there for me. And without the constant encouragement of Jack W.

Creech, Ph.D., this book would have never reached fruition.

Appreciation goes to Iris Temple, the friend of a friend, who led me to Alyss Dorese. And to my editor, Shelly Usen, whose pleasing manner made the difficult seem less difficult. A special thanks to my publisher, Gerald Sindell. His enthusiasm for the book renewed my energy for the finishing touches.

For their kind permission to use the photographs that proved so invaluable in telling this story, I am deeply grateful to Peter M. M. Sasson and the government of Kuwait.

As I laboriously gave birth to this book, Gilda Riccardi Froude, a dear friend, gave me unquestioned love and support even as she gave birth to my godson, James Giancarlo Liam Froude. This momentous event of new life gave me pause and led me to consider the personal effect the Iraqi invasion would have had on his parents' lives had he been born 20 years earlier. I pray that the son of John and Gilda Froude, along with millions of other sons and daughters of loving parents, will not be faced with the dilemma of war as we go into the twenty-first century.

To all of these people, thank you.

Preface

For twelve years I made my home in the Middle East. During this time I had come to know and love the people of the area, and the recurring violence there had never failed to pain me, for I knew firsthand the fate of the innocent people caught up in the explosive passions that plague the region. Aware that the West was bombarded with an onslaught of unflattering media images of gun-waving terrorists, I despaired that most people would summon up ghastly stock impressions of Arabs and have little sympathy for the plight of the real victims, the Arab people. And who could blame the citizens of the West for their distrust? These sinister caricatures were the only Arabs presented to them. But many Arabs were my friends; I knew them as human beings, just like the rest of us who populate this planet. They grow up filled with hope; they marry and raise their families; and they suffer when sorrow visits their hearth. And they die. But too many Arabs are dying young simply because they were born in the most tumultuous region on earth.

After witnessing countless upheavals over the course of the last decade, I had reached the conclusion that still more wars would be fought among the people I loved. There were simply too many unresolved ambitions, and too many instruments of death available, for the outcome to be peaceful. The land was seething with tanks, missiles, and military hardware. I had no crystal ball and could make no psychic predictions, but in my gut I knew that the mounting tensions would escalate until the day came when the entire world would become involved. That day came all too soon.

In June and July of 1990, I watched with mounting dread as Saddam Hussein, president of Iraq, began his verbal assaults on Kuwait. It was easy to conclude that with an army of one million, a shattered economy, and unrealized objectives, he was a menace. Having read everything published about him, I feared for the Kuwaitis. I called friends in Kuwait and Dubai (United Arab Emirates) who had fled the Lebanese war and told them it might be safer to go back and face the never-ending shelling of East Beirut than to wait on Saddam's armies. They laughed; they told me not to worry. It was all a bluff, they said. On the night of August 1, 1990, I settled in to watch one of my favorite television shows, "Nightline," and I was horrified to hear Ted Koppel announce the breaking story that Iraqi troops had invaded Kuwait and were racing toward Kuwait City. In an instant, my life was changed along with millions of others.

In the days that followed, I found I was unable to concentrate on a half-completed manuscript on the Middle East, so gripped was I by the unfolding drama. I listened intently to the press conferences called by Sheik Saud Nasir Al-Sabah, the Kuwaiti ambassador to the United States. I cried as I heard him appeal to all peoples of the world for help for his beleaguered land. I was so moved by his entreaties for help from any front, so drawn to his genteel manner, that I found myself at the typewriter telling him how I prayed for the recovery of his country and the safety of his people. I felt great sorrow for him and all the Kuwaitis, for I was fearful that once again the tyrants of the world would prevail. After mailing the letter to the ambassador, I continued to carefully analyze the political rhetoric spouted by world leaders. I felt with shame that the world would stand aside once again, just as it did during the massacres in Cambodia and China. I watched in despair as the refugees began to stream out of Kuwait and tell their tales of horror.

I called all my friends in the Middle East, running up phone bills that made AT&T stock rise, and still I felt I had to do something, to take some action that might help in some small way. Believing it was more important to write this book exposing the brutal events taking place in Kuwait, I reluctantly put aside the manuscript that had taken up all of my time for the past year. I vowed to talk to the people who had fled Kuwait in order to make their personal traumas known.

Even though the Middle East is like a second home to me, I knew it would be difficult to accomplish my goal with the necessary speed. I would require assistance in meeting the refugees. Although I do have a lot of friends who hold prominent positions in the region, somehow none of them seemed just right to help me in this project. Just as I was contemplating the momentous task ahead of me, the telephone rang. The ambassador from Kuwait was on the line. I told him that I was surprised that he had taken the time to respond to my letter. He asked me how anyone could fail to respond. After a few moments spent discussing the current situation, I told him about my plan to write a book on the Kuwaiti refugees, and I explained that I would need some help since time was scarce. By the time I hung up the phone, we had made plans for me to fly to Washington the following week with the ambassador and his staff.

Until his country was invaded by Iraq, few Americans had ever heard of Sheik Saud Nasir Al-Sabah. While appearing on numerous political talk shows to talk about the invasion, he impressed many Americans with his well-mannered, low-key approach to the crisis. Whereas the Iraqi ambassador, Mohammed Sadig Al-Mashat, insulted our intelligence with his blatant lies about the event, Nasir Al-Sabah calmly gave us the facts, then rested his case.

When I met the Kuwaiti ambassador in Washington, I had little personal knowledge of the man. Our meeting dealt with such basic matters as the route I planned to take in my travels and the assistance I would need in meeting his countrymen. Looking back, I have to confess I would never have guessed that he was confronted with a double crisis. Not only was his country attacked and brutally occupied, but the ambassador's wife, Awatif, his two daughters, and his grandchildren were trapped in Kuwait City. The ambassador himself was supposed to have been in Kuwait on August 2, 1990. His elder daughter had recently given birth in Kuwait City; since Washington virtually shuts down during August, he and his family were traveling home for the holidays to visit relatives and see their latest grandchild. When Saddam Hussein massed his troops on the Kuwaiti border, the ambassador canceled his plans and stayed with his sons in the capital. But, believing the assurances of Saddam Hussein and other Arab leaders, Al-Sabah allowed his wife and 16-year old daughter to return to Kuwait.

I noticed during my meeting with the ambassador that his eyes clouded over as I offered wishes for the well-being of his family. Even as he haltingly recounted his story, he downplayed his personal dilemma, concentrating instead on the plight of his country. But fear for his family accompanied me on my subsequent journey to the Middle East. I felt every nerve come alive as diplomats in Riyadh told me of the cash rewards Saddam Hussein had offered, as bounty, for members of the Al-Sabah family. I knew the ambassador's kin would be a prize indeed to the dictator. Every time I found an opportunity to speak off the record with members of the Kuwaiti government, I tried in vain to discover the fate of the ambassador's family.

From Washington I traveled to London and met Dr. Souad Al-Sabah, wife of Abdullah Al-Mubarak Al-Sabah, the only surviving son of Mubarak the Great. Souad and her family happened to be in London at the time of the invasion and now they were working around the clock to restore their country's sovereignty. Part of their work consisted of helping people such as myself get the story of the suffering Kuwaiti people in print or on the news. After hearing that I was dedicating the book to Kuwaitis killed during the invasion, with a special tribute to the Emir's brother, Sheik Fahd Al-Sabah, who had been among the first to die, Souad introduced me to his widow. I spent that first night in London meeting with Sheikher Fadila Al-Sabah. It was a night of sadness that I will never forget.

Souad and I made plans for my return through London as I rushed off to Cairo to meet with people who had recently escaped from Kuwait through the deserts of Saudi Arabia or Iraq and Jordan. Kuwait had been attacked so unexpectedly and invaded so quickly that mothers were separated from their children, infants were misplaced in hospitals, and husbands and wives were lost to each other forever.

In Cairo I met with business people, professionals, government workers, mothers, fathers—people who had left Kuwait only after they recognized the impossibility of surviving under the harsh new regime that ruled their once peaceful land. I heard more than pain in their voices. I also heard love, affection, pride, bravery, and determination to reclaim the land they loved.

In Saudi Arabia, my Sudanese driver, Sadeen, skillfully maneuvered his way around the jammed streets of Riyadh as I went from embassy offices to makeshift schoolhouses to hospitals to hear stories of suffering, sorrow, and helplessness resulting from Iraq's invasion. From Riyadh, I flew to the mountain retreat city of Taif, Saudi Arabia, where the exiled government of Kuwait waits and plans its return.

From the onset of the invasion, I planned this project as a way for the Kuwaiti people to speak directly to the world. This is not a book about diplomacy or military strategy used against Saddam Hussein. Such subjects were, and continue to be, covered in the news media.

During my travels and my talks with Kuwaiti citizens, I found that their country survived in the hearts and minds of its displaced, scattered people. This is their story, the story of the rape of Kuwait.

•

Kuwait: A Brief History

In the very best of times the interior of Arabia is a harsh environment. In a land devoid of trees (trees are so rare in the area that a bush causes great excitement and is generally called a tree) and with little water, the blazing sun quickly becomes man's worse adversary.

The camel made life possible in this barren land. The nomadic bedouin tribes that roamed Arabia in the eighteenth century depended solely upon the creature for their livelihood. Camels provided milk, food, clothing, and transport. The dung of the camel supplied fuel for their fires. The camel could survive on prickly bushes and meager amounts of water but some vegetation was necessary for life. When drought and famine visited the region in the early 1700s it became difficult for the camel to survive. Therefore, the bedouin tribes that roamed the area with their camels and goats scattered into various directions in search of water and foliage.

The Utab family, a division of the Anizah tribe of the Nejd (today's Saudi Arabia), migrated across the Arabian Peninsula and settled in what today is Kuwait City. It is not possible to fix an exact date for the establishment of Kuwait City but most researchers agree that the town facing the sea was built around 1716.

No one knows just why the location was selected, for it was one of the most merciless bits of land on earth. Certainly, the soil was no better than the sand that the Utabs had left. There was little drinkable water. Perhaps the bedouins grew weary and simply gave up searching for green grass and cool springs. For whatever the reason, the people of the tribe looked upon the waters of the Persian Gulf, noted the natural harbor and gave up their wandering ways. Although they remained strongly attracted to the desert by virtue of their past (for they were descended from desert nomads), they saw the possibilities of wealth in the sea. Thus, the settlers, ancestors of modern-day Kuwaitis, abandoned nomadism and became sailors and traders.

The Persian Gulf (called the Arabian Gulf by present-day Gulf countries) was rich in fish and pearls. In addition, there were ports from which Kuwaitis could export goods. Their nomadic culture quickly changed to one shaped by pearl-diving, seafaring international traders and travelers.

The settlers faced their new town toward the sea. They built their mud homes so close together that they looked like apartments. Their noisy bazaars were centers for community socialization.

In spite of the wealth of the sea, the Kuwaitis were depressingly poor. But the sting of poverty was removed by the fact they were more or less on the same level with other peoples of the area. Everyone lived in mud homes and ate the same bleak diet. Death came early and infant mortality was a serious problem. Travelers to the area wrote that the excessive poverty combined with the searing desert climate made life in Kuwait unbearable.

Like its neighbors, Kuwait was built upon a conservative, Islamic society. Smoking, drinking, and even singing were forbidden. However, the Kuwaitis' new residence by the sea influenced their behavior somewhat, and over the years the people became less stern and more spontaneous. As a result, Kuwaitis are known in the region for their tolerance of other religions, political movements, and practices different from their own.

Excluding a few events, daily life in Kuwait from 1716 until the discovery of oil in 1938 was monotonously predictable. The men put to sea in search of fish or pearls. Others travelled afar via desert camel caravans or ships to trade their wares. The women stayed in the homes and tended to the children and domestic duties, venturing out to the bazaars to purchase needed items of food or clothing and to socialize with other village women.

There are no surviving records of the first rulers of Kuwait. The earliest European travelers wrote that the town was ruled by a sheik but they made no mention of a family name. The first reference of the present day ruling family shows that a tribal council held in 1752 elected Sabah Bin Jaber of the Al-Sabah family to administer justice. Evidently, the Al-Sabah family was held in high esteem and thought to be fair-minded and impartial. Since the election of the first Al-Sabah, excluding one ugly incident in 1896, the family has more or less ruled peaceably.

In 1896, three brothers of the Al-Sabah family broke ranks over decision-making and power. Two full blood brothers, Mohammed and Jarrah, forced their half-brother, Mubarak, into the desert to manage the bedouins while they controlled the financial affairs of the city.

Already incensed over his limited influence, Mubarak learned of a plot by a rich Kuwaiti merchant, who was Iraqi by origin, to discharge the Al-Sabah family and become the ruler of Kuwait. This influential merchant, Yusuf Ibrahim, was closely associated with the Ottoman Governor of Basra (the Ottoman Empire had been created in 1300 and over the years had advanced their rule in the Arab world) and Mubarak feared that the Al-Sabah family would lose their rightful place as rulers. Convinced that his brothers were too cowardly to stop the conspiracy, Mubarak decided to kill them and assume leadership of the country.

One night in June, 1896, Mubarak, along with his sons, raided the home of his brothers. Mohammed was sleeping on the roof of the palace when Mubarak shot him. Surviving, Mohammed cried out for his brother to have mercy. The second shot killed him. Mubarak's other brother, Jarrah, was stabbed to death by Mubarak's son.

However, before Mubarak could consolidate his rule, Yusuf Ibrahim contacted the Governor of Basra in order to gain control of the area. Mubarak hastened to the Ottoman Governor of

Baghdad. In addition, both men sought the support of the British who were always interested in undermining Ottoman influence. In the end, Mubarak was more shrewd than Yusuf and he retained the power given his family in 1752. During Mubarak's rule (1896-1915), Kuwait grew more prosperous and as a result Mubarak became known as Mubarak the Great.

By the late 1800s, after six centuries of domination, the Ottoman Empire started to crumble. The empire, which at its height governed most of what we recognize today as Eastern Europe, along with vast holdings in Asia and the Middle East, was overextended and discontent was widespread with regard to overtaxation and conscription. The Ottomans manned their huge armies by unpopular and particularly cruel methods. Ottoman soldiers would appear without warning in small villages across the empire, gather all able-bodied men, and take them off to wars. Families were left to starve. Naturally, the citizens grew bitter and hostile. In addition, the Ottomans were in constant conflict with European powers for control of their Empire. After decades of political maneuvering and war, along with the difficulty of governing disgruntled citizens, the Ottoman

Empire weakened and became vulnerable to Western intervention.

The Imperial British Empire at its political peak with colonies spread across the globe and with a strong naval power, saw a long-awaited opportunity to gain a foothold in the Middle East. It was only natural that they sought out the rulers of the region in an attempt to exclude their bitter European rivals—France, Germany, and Russia—from advancing their cause in the area. When Germany attempted to extend the Berlin-Baghdad railway to the port of Kuwait, Great Britain intensified its efforts to influence Mubarak Al-Sabah. Mubarak's earlier, successful dealings with the British during his bid for power left him open to their seduction. As a result, Great Britain and Kuwait concluded an agreement in 1899 which gave the European country control of Kuwait's foreign affairs.

In 1914, when the First World War broke out, the Ottomans joined forces with Great Britain's enemy, Germany. In order to protect their Middle Eastern interests, Great Britain established a protectorate over the tiny state of Kuwait. World War I rang the death knell for the Ottoman Empire. The victorious European allies—Great Britain, France, and Russia—partitioned the Ottoman territories with a series of wartime agreements that paved the way for numerous border disputes in the twentieth century.

In 1922, after tiring of continuous bickering among the governments of Iraq, Saudi Arabia, and Kuwait, Sir Percy Cox, the British High Commissioner in Iraq, simply took pen in hand and made a new map. He gave some of Kuwait's territory to Iraq and some to Saudi Arabia. He gave a bit of Saudi land to Iraq. Not surprisingly, no one was happy. When the Kuwaiti ruler, Ahmad Al-Sabah, questioned the fairness of the decision, Sir Percy informed him that due to Kuwait's small size and status, Kuwait would have to adhere to the wishes of its larger neighbors. Iraq, not satisfied with just a small amount of Kuwaiti and Saudi territory, insisted upon a larger bite. Saudi Arabia's ruler, Abul Aziz Al-Saud, was furious with the loss of any land at all. Yet, due to the might and influence of the British Empire, the borders remained fairly stable until the great wealth of oil generated rumblings of greed.

In 1938, oil was discovered in the Burgan oilfield about 80 miles from the Saudi border. Even so, the effects were not immediately felt due to the outbreak of World War II, during which exploration and production were halted.

On June 30, 1946, the oil tap was turned. Kuwait has never been the same since.

The economic boom arrived; oil money quickly transformed Kuwait into a sophisticated modern state. The Kuwaiti people embraced the deluge and developed an advanced economic and social welfare system.

On June 19, 1961, the British government announced that Kuwait was fully independent. On June 25, the Iraqi government claimed Kuwait as an inherent part of their country. The Iraqis argued that Kuwait had belonged to the Ottoman Empire along with Iraq and was governed under the same province; therefore, it belonged with Iraq. The Iraqi prime minister stated that ethnically and socially Iraq and Kuwait were as one. To further their claim, the Iraqis massed troops along the border. Abdul Allah Al-Sabah, the ruler of Kuwait, appealed to the British for help and in July, the British landed forces on Kuwait's beaches. On July 20, the Arab League, formed in 1945, embraced Kuwait as a member and refuted the Iraqi claim. The Iraqis withdrew their troops but did not drop their claim until October, 1963.

Although the threat of a takeover by Iraq continued to remain a factor in Iraqi-Kuwaiti relations, relative calm prevailed in Kuwait until the late 1970's. During this period, Kuwait became the most open society in the Gulf, with full education and work possibilities for women. Unlike most Arab countries, the Kuwaitis welcomed the homeless Palestinians. By 1990, over 450,000 Palestinians lived and worked in Kuwait. Favored by many Asians as a work haven, the country literally hummed with activity. Many third world workers said that Kuwait gave them hope for a prosperous future.

While their neighbors, Iran and Iraq, spent their newfound oil wealth on arms, the Kuwaiti government emphasized the needs of the people and provided education, jobs, homes, and health care. When the oil money overflowed, the Kuwaitis formed committees and channelled their extra funds into works of charity worldwide. Orphanages in Lebanon, dams in Africa, and schools in Palestine benefited from Kuwaiti generosity.

Kuwait's peaceful era ended with the downfall of the Shah of Iran on January 16, 1979. The new Islamic Republic of Iran was headed by Ruhollah Khomeini, who was awarded the title of Ayatollah (which means sign from God) by an Islamic jurist. Suddenly, an angry revolution led by a religious fundamentalist confronted

Kuwait. Determined to overthrow the leaders of all Arab states and replace their governments with revolutionary Islamic republics, the Ayatollah began a concerted campaign against the Kuwaitis. With Islamic rhetoric, suicide bombings, and plane hijackings, the Ayatollah sought to dismantle the facade of the peaceable nation.

The hint of worse to come arrived when Iraq invaded Iran in September, 1980. Caught between two aggressive neighbors, the Kuwaitis backed what they considered the lesser evil, Saddam Hussein's Iraq.

The days turned into months and the months into years and still the determined Iranians and Iraqis fought on with apocalyptic fury. The Kuwaitis, terrified of an Iranian Islamic fundamentalist victory, poured billions of dollars into Saddam Hussein's war-drained coffers and pleaded his cause in the West. There is little doubt that without the help of Kuwait and other moderate Gulf states, Saddam Hussein would have been toppled by Ayatollah Khomeini.

The war finally ended in August, 1988, with scores of victims but no clearcut victor.

The Kuwaitis assumed the danger had passed. Iran had been neutralized by eight years of bloodletting and Saddam Hussein was thought to be their grateful friend.

The Kuwaiti people started the year 1990 with optimism. The long war between Iran and Iraq was over and the Kuwaiti people were anxious to look ahead and forget the somber decade-long dread of regional tensions. In spite of the past huge economic outlay to Iraq's war efforts, the Kuwait Fund for Arab Economic Development continued to maintain its lending programs. There was talk of concentrated attention on the deteriorating situation regarding the continuing call for a Palestinian homeland. Most importantly, there was a growing movement to reinstate the Parliament.

In July, 1990, just as people were happily anticipating their long-awaited summer holidays, Saddam Hussein made a call for Kuwait to lower their oil production. He charged that Kuwait was overproducing in order to ruin Iraq's economy. An accusation was made that Kuwait was slant drilling and stealing Iraqi oil from the Rumaila oilfields. Hussein brought up the old subject of ports. He demanded a favorable lease for the Warba and Bubiyan islands. Iraq's 26-mile shoreline had been ruined by the war with Iran (ships were sunk in the harbor, thereby making it virtually useless). Hussein reminded the Kuwaitis that scores of young Iraqi men had lost their lives in the war with Iran, the war that he claimed was fought to protect Kuwaitis from the Iranians. (Actually the war was fought over disputed territory between Iran and Iraq.) Hussein claimed that the Kuwaitis were ungrateful for the tremendous sacrifices made by Iraq, and, while he was on the subject, suggested that the twelve to fifteen billion dollar loan from Kuwait for war purposes should be forgiven.

Though shaken, the Kuwaitis could not believe Saddam Hussein was serious or would invade their country. They felt the bond of friendship and family with their neighbor country. Kuwaitis and Iraqis had intermarried, they helped each other in times of need, they were brothers.

The Kuwaitis watched in quiet dismay as Hussein moved 100,000 men from his 1,000,000-man army on their border. The leaders of Saudi Arabia, Jordan, and Egypt grew nervous at the hawkish moves of the Iraqi leader. Presidents and kings flew to Baghdad and conferred with Hussein. Hope for a diplomatic settlement was kept alive by assurances from the Iraqi leader that he would not resort to military action.

Saudi Arabia's King Fahd arranged a special meeting in Jedda, Saudi Arabia, to resolve the difficulties once and for all. The meeting was not successful. The Iraqis made unreasonable demands and then marched out of the meeting in protest when their demands were not met. The Kuwaitis were concerned but still confident that a peaceful solution would be found.

Following developments closely, the Kuwaiti ambassador to Washington cancelled his planned trip home but felt no apprehension as he watched his wife and 16-year-old daughter board a flight to Kuwait.

At dawn, August 2, 1990, Saddam Hussein commanded his army to invade Kuwait.

In 1773, a plague arrived from Baghdad and almost wiped out the entire population of Kuwait. Two hundred and seventeen years later, another plague arrived from Baghdad. Somehow, this latest plague seems worse.

•

Khalid and Wafa Al-Khayat

Khalid and his wife, Wafa, were counting the days until September. They had given little thought to the Iraqi dictator or his menacing army for they had their hearts set on a dream shared by most young couples: a new home. Khalid and Wafa had been married for nine years and had been living with his parents. Finally, the home that they had been waiting for since they married was going to be ready in September. Now they would be able to move into a home of their own.

As far as Khalid was concerned, August 2, 1990 was just another normal day. He worked as an aircraft engineer with Kuwaiti Airlines and generally travelled a great deal. But this was a Thursday and he only had to work a half day. (In the Middle East, Thursdays are the same as our Saturdays, since Friday is the Moslem day of worship.)

On the way to work, Khalid thought the city seemed strange. The streets were busier than usual for a Thursday. Suddenly his car started to jerk. He got out to check and see what was the matter but couldn't find anything wrong. The car started to jerk again without him inside or the motor running. Then he realized that he heard bombing! He saw some high-ranking Kuwaiti soldiers running all around; he stopped some of them and asked what was going on. They told him to report immediately to the air force base.

Since Kuwait has such a small population (1990 census: 826,586 Kuwaitis with a little over half being male) all males from age 18 to 30 are required to be in the reserves.

At this point, Khalid was more confused than frightened. He knew something bad was happening but had no way of knowing exactly what it was. At the base he saw that the Iraqis were bombing the runways. He rushed inside and saw a large group of young Kuwaiti men. No one knew anything more than that Kuwait was being attacked by Iraq. Searching frantically for a radio, they finally located a small set. They listened, but did not receive any worthwhile information. The station was playing Kuwaiti national songs and occasionally would break in to appeal to the men of the nation by stating: "Join the call to duty. Your country is calling you! Report to the nearest military unit!" No one knew what to do so the men stayed at the base and took turns using the phones to call their families to see if they were right.

Wafa and her in-laws were horrified at what was happening. Hearing from Khalid relieved their tension somewhat. Khalid assured his family that it would be over quickly and everything would return to normal. He didn't want them upset.

Meanwhile, the base was surrounded by Iraqi tanks and Khalid and his colleagues were defenseless. A few of the uniformed officers had handguns but everyone else was unarmed. They were helpless in the face of the heavily armed Iraqi army; they simply had to sit and wait for whatever God had in store for them. By this time, the men in uniforms had an inkling of the harm that was in store for them and many started stripping off their uniforms and trying to escape in their underwear.

The Iraqis sat outside and waited. The Kuwaitis sat inside and waited. The waiting game went on until the following day. By this time (Friday afternoon), the men were weary. The tension had been building. No one had slept. There was some water but no food. During the day they heard airplanes taking off from the runways and could not imagine who or what they were. Much later they found out that some death-defying Kuwaiti air force pilots had slipped out and taken Kuwaiti jets to Saudi Arabia. Miraculously, they made it.

Recognizing the futility of just sitting inside the base, the Kuwaiti military officers surrendered to the Iraqis at 1:00 P.M. on Friday afternoon. Suddenly the tanks started moving and the troops marched toward the men. Certain that the Iraqis were going to kill everyone, Khalid found some comfort in the fact that he was with friends. He and 25 of his friends stayed together for moral support.

The conquering Iraqis were businesslike and abrupt. They told the men to go outside. Then they searched the base and brought out the people who were hiding. They distributed everyone according to rank. Sensing the fear of the captives, the Iraqis assured the men they would be allowed to go home. After a while they did release everyone who did not have on a uniform. Eight hundred Kuwaitis were held and Khalid was one of them. He tried to explain to the Iraqis that his uniform was that of an aircraft engineer for Kuwaiti Airlines, but the Iraqis told him that didn't matter. He had to stay. In their apprehension and disappointment

Khalid and the rest of the men were silent. They didn't know what the Iraqis had in store for them.

Khalid and the other 799 men were transported by truck to a fenced-in fire station. They were kept outside in the hot sun. Although they had not eaten for nearly two days, no one complained of hunger. They were numb and exhausted and ready for anything—even death.

By this time Kuwaiti families were hunting their husbands, sons and brothers and word got out that the Iraqis had imprisoned a lot of men at the fire station. Wafa and her mother-in-law went to look. There were two missing men in their family—Khalid and his 25-year-old brother, Bega. Bega, a civilian petroleum engineer, was at work at the time of the invasion. He called his family during the invasion and shouted that they were surrounded by Iraqi soldiers and one man had been shot. That was the last the family heard of him. When Wafa and her mother-in-law found Khalid at the fire station they began to cry hysterically from relief. They gave him the little amount of food they had brought with them. When they had to leave, Khalid feared he would never see them again and was bitterly disappointed that he could not go with them. Khalid took the food and divided it with his friends.

The men were instructed by Kuwaiti officers to be calm and do nothing to excite the Iraqis who were becoming increasingly nervous and jumpy. The Kuwaitis with money started bribing the Iraqi soldiers. About forty Kuwaitis managed to escape in this manner. The Iraqi soldiers did not know that the Iraqi government had brought the value of the Kuwaiti dinar down to the same value as the Iraqi dinar and were under the impression they were getting a lot of money, when in fact, they were making little. A few of the younger men tried to slip away but they were caught and beaten severely. At one time a young man, about seventeen, became hysterical and started screaming and crying. He completely lost control. Khalid and other men surrounded him and tried to calm him for they were fearful that the Iraqis would take him away or worse, shoot him.

On the third morning, the Iraqis took all the officers away. No one knew what would happen but it didn't look good. By now, the lack of food and the extreme heat were making life more than miserable for the prisoners. Khalid felt they would be moved next, perhaps to

Baghdad, and began to get concerned for his life.

At about 6:30 A.M. on Monday morning he saw a man bribe his way inside the fire station to hunt for a relative. Khalid went to meet him to see if he could help. They looked everywhere for the man's relative, only to find that he had escaped earlier. Khalid asked the man to claim him instead as his relative. After all, the man had already paid a bribe and his relative was safe. It was Khalid's only chance. Luckily, the man agreed and after a nervous exit past the guards, Khalid found himself free.

He went with the man to check on his relative. They found him at a friend's house. Then the man offered to take Khalid home.

Wafa screamed with joy when Khalid walked in the door. After finding out about his family, Khalid showered, ate a big meal, and then lay down for a much needed nap. Afterwards, listening to the radio, he found out that the Iraqis were rounding up a lot of men. Since he had escaped, Khalid felt that they might come looking for him. After a family conference, it was decided that the entire family should go to stay at a relative's house.

Meanwhile, the Kuwaiti people started gathering in homes and putting up their own resistance. To confuse the Iraqis, they removed all street signs and house numbers. Khalid removed street and house signs around his neighborhood. Then he told his family that he planned to leave Kuwait. The Iraqis, who had stolen the Kuwaiti Airlines fleet but did not know how to operate all the equipment, were gathering up all persons trained on the 767s and airbuses. Since Khalid was an aircraft engineer, he knew it was just a matter of time until they started looking for him.

Khalid and Wafa made plans to leave but could not convince Khalid's parents or other family members to go with them. Khalid's mother refused to leave until she could find out about Bega. Wafa tried to contact her family but the phone lines were cut. Wafa left her father, two brothers, and two sisters in Kuwait (two sisters were out of the country when the invasion occurred).

Khalid and Wafa left with a relative who owned a four-wheel drive. They left with very little money. They had managed to save $30,000, but that was lost because the Iraqis had looted all the banks. Khalid was careful to take all his educational and work certificates, since he felt he had to start his life from scratch. He felt pretty hopeless as he left. He felt Kuwait was finished and it was an awful feeling. He surveyed the damage done and he saw a country destroyed.

They were on the highway only fifteen minutes before they had to take the desert road. Iraqi soldiers were everywhere. When the soldiers saw them they started shooting in the air and forced them to stop. Khalid was prepared for anything. The soldier told them they could not leave and said he would have to shoot them if they continued. Khalid's relative got out and bribed the soldier. Then the soldier told them the way to go.

After about two and one-half hours they spotted Saudi soldiers. The Saudis welcomed them and offered them food, water, and gas for the car. Khalid looked at his watch. It was 10:00 P.M. on August 16. He had spent fourteen days under the Iraqis.

By a stroke of good luck, Khalid decided to go to Bahrain. There he ran into an old friend from the airline who told him that Kuwaiti Airlines was going to open with the few planes they had. He asked Khalid if he wanted to go to work. Khalid eagerly jumped at the chance. He was rehired and sent to Cairo. He would live and work there until he could return to his country.

Wafa had a difficult time finding out about her family due to the cut phone lines. Khalid's family received the news first about Wafa's brother. They called Khalid and told him what had happened. Wafa's younger brother, who was only 22, had joined the resistance. He was going out to meet some of his friends when the Iraqis took him and shot him. Due to the circumstances, it was impossible to find out the details of his death. Khalid and Wafa were told quite simply that he was dead and buried.

Unable to comprehend her great loss, Wafa spends a lot of time staring out the window with tears rolling down her cheeks. Unconsciously she wrings her hands. It's hard to believe such a young and happy boy is dead. Shot to death.

•

Nusaiba and Talal Al-Essa

If anyone had told Nusaiba that she would ever leave Kuwait she would have laughed in his face. After the invasion, she and her sister would sit and watch other Kuwaitis leave, upset that Kuwaitis would leave their country and just let the Iraqis take over.

Nusaiba was educated as an economics major, but found that she preferred being a wife and mother. She felt so blessed and fortunate that she stressed to her eight children the importance of sharing their good fortune. In spite of a large family, she found time to work in two committees that built schools and hospitals and helped families in other countries less prosperous than her own. Nusaiba loved her busy, active lifestyle.

Her husband, Talal, had become quite wealthy. He was the Ferrari dealer in Kuwait and with the proceeds from the sale of oil, a lot of Kuwaitis could afford to buy Ferraris. Talal provided well for his family and found much joy in raising a large number of children and being able to provide well for them. He had an intelligent and beautiful wife who was a wonderful mother. All his children were healthy. What more could any man want? But Talal felt differently than his wife after the invasion. He felt responsible for the safety of his large family. He was nervous from the first moment he saw six helicopters flying. It was Thursday, August 2, the morning of the invasion. He called his wife and children to come out and look. Kuwaitis were not used to seeing helicopters.

Nusaiba and the children were curious but not afraid. They saw that the helicopters were black. One of the children pointed out the Iraqi flag and they knew something was wrong. Like most Kuwaitis, they dashed into the house to turn on the news.

From that first day, Nusaiba wanted to stay in Kuwait and Talal wanted to leave. When the barbaric behavior of the invaders became known, Talal became frantic with worry. The Iraqis were taking away young men; Talal had an 18-year-old son, Naif. The Iraqis were raping women; Talal had a beautiful wife and six daughters. Nusaiba did not think of giving in to the invaders, but Talal could think of little else than to leave.

Then one day their eldest child, Naif, called his mother and asked her to come and talk to him. He told her that is was commendable that she wanted to stay and understandable that she did not want to leave her home and country. But he asked her to think about her husband. He said, "Father is not eating and he is losing a lot of weight. He is getting sick from worry over his daughters. What can we do if the Iraqis come? We cannot protect ourselves against guns. I am afraid this worry will kill my father. Please think about this and the health of your husband."

Nusaiba looked at her husband and saw him losing weight and lines forming on his face. She saw two of her daughters, one 10 and the other 15, were so frightened of the Iraqis that they slept fully clothed with their heads covered. She remembered how the Iraqis came and took her sister's 22-year-old son away for no reason. He was very innocent and had never even held a gun. His fate was unknown. Would her 18-year-old son be next?

When Nusaiba finally decided to leave, it couldn't be quickly enough. She told her husband and children that they were leaving, immediately! She put one huge suitcase on the floor and told the children that each one could put one favorite item inside. The children were rushing around grabbing favorite toys and then discarding them and running for another. Ten people were leaving the only home they had ever known. No one could decide upon one item. In the end, they left with hardly anything at all.

Nusaiba's brother had wanted to leave since the invasion. His wife was eight months pregnant and his nights were sleepless with worry. The Iraqis were closing the hospitals and how could he deliver a baby? What if something went wrong? When Nusaiba and her family decided to leave they contacted her brother and he came over with his heavily expectant wife to join the exodus.

Filled with foreboding about meeting up with Iraqis along the way, Nusaiba read the Koran to her family to calm their fears. In many instances, Iraqis took away young men at the border to their death or imprisonment and dragged young women out and raped them. She knew she had to trust in God to deliver her family safely. In their haste, the family had failed to bring items to bribe the Iraqis but were relieved to find that Nusaiba's brother had remembered the greed of their invaders. When the Iraqis stopped them, Nusaiba's brother was driving the first car. He bribed the enemy and told them that the car behind was with him. In this way, the family of Talal and Nusaiba Al-Essa reached Cairo safely.

Even so, Talal is still nervous and frightened. He has a large family to feed and support and the Iraqis have taken his livelihood. They stole every car in his showroom and then destroyed the building. He will have to start at the bottom and he is anxious. Where his life had been full of promise and time was always short, now he has nothing but time. His youngest children do not understand why they cannot go home and play with their toys. His seven year-old son, Ahmad, wants his desk so he can do his homework. Talal pretends that he is on a two-month holiday and will soon go back to a free Kuwait. It is the only way he can cope.

•

Fuad Al-Hashem

Fuad Al-Hashem is what we call in America a late father. He was scared to death to get married but once he met a certain Lebanese woman he managed to overcome his fear and settle down to marital bliss. As a result of the union, he is the doting father of Farah, a two-year-old baby daughter. It was due to this great love of his daughter that Fuad fled through the desert to Saudi Arabia and safety.

Before the invasion, Fuad made his living as a journalist who wrote political articles for a Kuwaiti newspaper. At least that is what he did in the mornings. After lunch, he would go to his toy store which he managed in a Disneyland-type park in Kuwait.

A political writer, Fuad became concerned earlier in the summer when Iraqi newspapers, on the orders of Saddam Hussein, suddenly began their harsh verbal bashing of Kuwait. He followed the Iraqi papers closely, feeling they were part of the emotional build-up designed to arouse the anger of the Iraqi people. After all the talk about oil and money along with the Iraqi troop movements, Fuad thought that there was going to be a "little invasion" resulting in loss of land and an oilfield or two. Never in his wildest dreams did he suspect he was in danger of losing his country.

On the morning of the invasion, Fuad woke up at 7:30 and turned on his television to listen to the FM music. He stood in a stupor when he say a sign on the screen that said "Long Live the Kuwaiti Revolution!" It took him about two minutes to force his body to move. Another shock followed as an Iraqi screamed on the air that there was a Kuwaiti revolution and asked people to come and help. At this, Fuad went into high gear, threw on his clothes without showering or shaving, and jumped in his car, driving away without even waking his wife. He saw Iraqi troops by the thousands swarming all over Kuwait City. His first reaction was, Kuwait is finished and now I have to deal with these Iraqis! By this time he heard bombing and shooting and thought he'd go home and put on Western clothes, as a safety precaution.

His wife was still asleep so he changed clothes and went back out. As a journalist, he was trained to see everything firsthand. He stopped first at the compound of the Emir. He couldn't believe his eyes. The whole neighborhood (the Emir lived in a compound with other members of his family) had been burned to the ground. Only the wall surrounding the compound was still standing and it was burning. While he was looking, two planes flew over, targeting the compound and dropping bombs. One of Fuad's neighbors, a military officer, had been taken to the ruined compound by the Iraqis and told that all of Kuwait would be destroyed in the same manner if the military resisted. The officer was allowed to approach the compound; there he saw the hands and feet of women and children sticking out of the rubble.

As Fuad drove away, he had to swerve around the dead bodies in the streets. The Iraqi tanks had just rolled over the bodies of the Kuwaitis, deliberately smashing their faces.

About this time, Fuad began to think about food for his family. He turned around and made a dash to the supermarket. The supermarkets were crammed with panic-stricken people. Fuad panicked along with the crowd. All he could think of was his daughter and her favorite food, chicken dipped in catsup. Fuad found himself rushing from store to store trying to find chicken. He managed to get catsup but no chicken. He had worked himself into a frenzy over this need to find chicken and neglected to buy anything else. On the road he spotted a chicken delivery truck and managed to get the driver to pull over. Fuad ran toward him and bought three dozen chickens.

Relieved, Fuad drove home with the chickens. At the front door he was met by his wife who was crying and screaming and hanging on to their baby and asking what they were going to do. Fuad calmed her down somewhat and they made a shelter in the basement with beds, blankets, food, and water.

About this time, a doctor from the hospital called and told Fuad to come and pick up his mother who was being treated for a heart condition. The Iraqis were raiding the hospitals and all the patients had to go home. When Fuad arrived at the hospital, he was shocked at the number of dead people. The morgue was filled to capacity and dead bodies were stacked everywhere.

Fuad found his mother and put her in the car to take her home. He was more upset than ever. His doctor friend had advised him what to do for his baby if Iraq engaged in chemical warfare. Fuad decided right then and there that the invasion was not a joke; he knew he could never bear to watch his baby die from chemicals.

On the way home, he decided he had to leave Kuwait as quickly as possible and made his plans. He dropped his mother off at his home and then went from one gas station to another, collecting gas for the escape across the desert.

On one of his trips, Fuad was approached by a group of Iraqi soldiers. They told him they were starving and asked if Fuad knew of a good restaurant. Fuad agreed to take them to an Indian restaurant he liked. While driving, he asked the soldiers why they had come to Kuwait. The soldiers declared that they had been invited by the people of Kuwait to depose the Emir. Fuad told them that was news to him, but the soldiers were certain that was the case. They were sorry that they missed capturing the Emir and the Crown Prince but happy they had Kuwait.

On their way to the restaurant, an Iraqi officer spotted the soldiers in the car with Fuad and forced Fuad to pull over. The officer started screaming at the soldiers that they should not be in a civilian car and that Fuad might be a terrorist. The soldiers leapt out and search Fuad's car but found nothing. They complained to the officer that they were starving. They had not eaten in days and had very little water. The officer screamed at them some more and told them not to do it again. Fuad dropped them off at the restaurant and continued on his way.

Fuad decided to go to his toy store in the amusement park area to see if there was any money left in the safe. He did not know if the Iraqis had gotten there yet or not. Luckily he found the cash in the safe and headed back to his home. He was ready to leave Kuwait.

On the way back home, an Iraqi soldier forced Fuad to pull off the read. When Fuad let down his car window, the cold air of the air conditioner hit the Iraqi in the face. The Iraqi screamed at Fuad, "You Kuwaiti you! Sitting in air conditioning while I suffer in the hot sun! Get out! Get out!" Fuad got out and stood there helpless while the Iraqi drove off with his supplies of gas and what little money he had.

Fuad made his way home and decided he would have to escape in his jeep. He knew it would be rough and bumpy for his wife and child but now he had no choice.

When Fuad walked in his front door, he told his wife they were leaving within the hour. The situation in Kuwait was getting worse by the minute. His mother had gone over to his sister's house so he called her to tell her he was leaving and asked if she wanted to go with him. His mother screamed to him that he was crazy and then hung up the phone. At noon, the worst part of the day for travel, Fuad gathered up some cheese, milk, and bread for the baby and took off.

Near the Saudi border he was stopped at a checkpoint by Iraqi soldiers. Fuad's wife started to cry and told the soldiers that they had to leave because of their baby. Fuad offered money to one of the soldiers to let them pass, but the soldier threw the money back at him and said it was shit money, just like Iraqi money. Fuad tried to give him his watch but the Iraqi glanced at it disdainfully and then threw it back. He told Fuad the watch was cheap and he didn't want it. Fuad kept talking to the man to try to get through but the man got tired of hearing him and started shooting in the air, right next to Fuad's ear. At the sound of the gun, Fuad's wife and baby started screaming, and Fuad took off as fast as he could. He told his wife they would just have to go through the desert.

Fuad will never forget the sights he saw in the desert. He saw entire families dead. He saw abandoned cars with their doors open. He saw a dead man with his head on the steering wheel and his wife beside him. He saw babies trying to crawl under their mothers' clothing. He spotted a car filled with women and children and one lone man outside the car trying to free it from the desert sand. The man was digging frantically but the sand would fill back quicker than he could dig. Fuad decided to stop and help. He told the man that pushing the car with his jeep might hurt the car, but the man did not care; he was stuck in the middle of the desert with women and children. After about six minutes the car was free. Delighted, the man jumped in and roared off with his large family.

Everywhere cars were stuck in the desert sand. Fuad knew that if he and his family had escaped in his car, their fate would have been the same.

For the first time he was grateful to the Iraqi who stole his car. His air-conditioned car would have been their coffin.

Fuad's escape through the desert lasted hours. The ordeal took its toll. His wife was crying. His child would scream every time he hit a bump. Devastated at his inability to help more people, Fuad had to start covering his eyes with his hands.

Suddenly Fuad saw an armed Iraqi soldier standing in the middle of the desert. He was frightened. He slowed and looked at the soldier to see what he was going to do. The soldier, who was about 45, looked Fuad right in the eyes, and pointed his gun toward Saudi Arabia. He was showing Fuad the correct way.

The happiest moment of Fuad's life was when he saw a Saudi soldier on the border. The second happiest was when he got into a tub of water. Once safely across the border, however, Fuad felt that if there were chemical warfare his baby would still not be safe. So, he made his way to Cairo to wait out the crisis from a distance.

After his escape, Fuad reflected on the condition of life for his fellow Kuwaitis still suffering under Iraqi rule, especially those who were ill. He recalled the day in 1984 he had visited a friend in the hospital. Fuad had heard a child screaming and, upon investigating, he found that child having dialysis. He was told that the child needed a kidney transplant but that Kuwait did not have a transplant program. Moved, Fuad began working that day to rectify the problem. By the time of the invasion, six years later, the Kuwaiti Transplant Society had arranged transplants for 100 persons. When

Fuad heard that the Iraqis were now stealing all the dialysis machines and hospital equipment, he knew that a lot of people would die painful deaths. He is concerned about his family that stayed behind and mourns the loss of his country that, within hours, had just disappeared.

Now in Cairo, Fuad is worried about how to support his wife and child and stunned by the total devastation of his way of life. He masks his concern with a smile, humor, and good nature. I interviewed many such Kuwaitis. I cried a lot. I only laughed once and that was with Fuad Al-Hashem.

•

Azza Salah Abd Eimotlai

Azza, an Egyptian social worker, and her two
young children were at home on the morning of
the invasion when her brother-in-law burst into
the house yelling, "The Iraqis are here!" Azza
was puzzled as to what he meant and asked
him what on earth the Iraqis were doing in
Kuwait. Her brother-in-law yelled out something about tanks and he pushed her toward
the window. Sure enough, there were tanks on
the beach.

Azza called her supervisor at the Handicapped Home for Children. Her supervisor was
excited; she could hear bombing and see hand-
to-hand fighting between Iraqis and Kuwaitis.
The Kuwaiti Police Academy was close by the
Handicapped Home and there was heavy fighting at the academy. Now Azza realized the seriousness of the situation. She was supposed to
report to work at 1:00 that afternoon and told
her supervisor she would try to make it.

Shortly after, Azza's husband, Adel, came
back home. He had left for work early in the

morning, but the Iraqis would not let him pass and told him to return home. Azza asked Adel to walk out to the Iraqi tanks and ask the soldiers what they were doing in Kuwait. Adel walked out to the beach area and chatted with some of the Iraqi soldiers. The Iraqis informed Adel that the Kuwaitis had asked them to come and help them get rid of the Emir and asked why the Kuwaitis were not out swimming. Adel came back laughing and told Azza that the Iraqis just couldn't understand why they were not on the beach, it being such a beautiful day and all.

When Azza told Adel she was planning to go to work, he became angry with her. Azza told him she simply had to go. There were over 300 children at the Home and Azza loved each and every one of them. She knew that the bombing would frighten them. She was also concerned that many employees would not be able to get through the fighting and these children could not look after themselves.

Azza called her supervisor back and told her she shouldn't let any of the employees leave since the next shift probably would not be able to get through. But Azza assured her she would be coming in no matter what. Azza had worked at the Home for seven years and she felt a tremendous responsibility for the welfare of the children.

Adel tried to take her to work but they were stopped by Iraqi soldiers who would not let them pass. Azza told them she worked in a hospital for children and she had to get through. The Iraqis told her to go home and celebrate: today Kuwait was free. They told her she could go to work the next morning but she had a holiday on that day to celebrate her freedom.

The next day, Azza finally made it to work. Her husband was still upset but he had accepted her decision. Azza cried all the way to work. She had to pass the area between the National Guard and the Missile Defense. Evidently there had been vicious fighting in the area for everything was burning and destroyed and bodies littered the ground. She was overcome by the senseless waste of life and property.

Azza was standing in the reception area of the Home when Iraqi soldiers burst in. She was afraid for the children so she ran to the automatic doors and met the soldiers there. She asked them what they wanted and told them that only handicapped children were in the building. The soldiers came in and destroyed the pictures of the Emir and the Crown Prince and then they asked Azza for money. Azza told them that they did not keep money in the Home, but the soldiers insisted that they must have some money. Finally she convinced them otherwise and they left.

As the shooting and the bombing became more intense, Azza spent most of her time calming hysterical children. After three days, their food supply started getting low and they had to ration. Some of the children required special food because they could not swallow and this food was running out. There were also not enough employees or volunteers to take care of so many helpless children. Azza and her supervisor started calling families and asking them to come and pick up their children. The situation was deteriorating rapidly.

Azza and the nurses knew that the Iraqi soldiers would come back. They put the handicapped children with the worst disabilities out in the front to play. When the soldiers spotted these children, they ran away. By this method, they were able to protect themselves from the soldiers.

Some of the children started chanting "Saddam die, Saddam die." No one knew where the children had learned this chant but they had to keep these children away from any possible contact with the soldiers or they knew there would be repercussions.

Finally an Iraqi man, who called himself the new Kuwaiti undersecretary, came to the Home to speak with the supervisor. He tried to act nice and asked them if they needed anything. He informed them that the Iraqis would now be in charge of Kuwait. When the supervisor told him that they needed 3,000 meals for the children immediately, he went away shocked and never returned.

By this time, Azza had stayed at the Home for three days while Adel kept their two children. Adel and his brother insisted that they leave Kuwait. They knew that life was going to be bad under the Iraqis. Azza's younger brother, who had arrived one week prior to the invasion for his first job in Kuwait, was also anxious to leave. Although Azza regarded Kuwait as her real home (she had been educated in Kuwait and lived there since she was fourteen) she told her husband that she would leave when the Egyptian Embassy advised all Egyptians to leave.

As the days passed, violence between the Kuwaitis and the Iraqis became more common. One day Azza went to the supermarket. There were two Iraqis inside stealing food. A Kuwaiti man came in and pretended to be looking at the food. Suddenly he pulled out a gun with a silencer and he shot and killed both Iraqi soldiers. Everyone in the market ran out. Another Iraqi soldier came in and saw the two dead Iraqis. He took his machine gun and shot up the store.

When Azza heard about the American response to the invasion and the enormous military build-up, she realized there might be a big war on Kuwaiti soil. She started to worry about the safety of Heba, her six-year-old daughter, and Edel, her three-year-old son. She finally agreed with her husband to leave Kuwait but she dreaded telling her supervisor and cringed at the thought of leaving the children.

Azza's supervisor understood completely and tried to make Azza feel less guilty. Although the status of the children was uncertain and the food supplies were nearly gone, the morale of the workers was good. The children were acting wild but the lack of personal care and unregulated schedules explained their behavior. Reluctantly and painfully, Azza made her good-byes.

Azza was unwilling to risk the Saudi desert. She had heard of too many deaths. It was decided that the family would drive through

Iraq, a decision that Azza would question many times over the course of the long and often arduous journey.

The Iraqis shocked Azza. They were dreadfully poor and ragged. As they drove through the cities, Iraqi women and children would try to stop the cars and steal their belongings. Azza found them to be exceptionally rude. In one frightening instance, Adel stopped for gas. When he went inside to pay, an Iraqi man came right up to the car and stuck his face close to Azza. She screamed at him and told him he should be ashamed. She asked him if he had any sisters and if so would he want a man to look at them in such a manner. The Iraqi screamed back at Azza that he did not hurt her but he moved away nevertheless.

Just when they were almost out of Iraq, they lost sight of Adel's brother, who was following in his car. They waited and finally the brother arrived by bus. The Iraqis had stolen his car. Adel was so incensed that he went back to help retrieve his brother's car and Azza was left alone with the children to drive the last fifty miles to Jordan. She was not concerned since it was only a few miles, but when she arrived at the Iraqi/Jordanian border she was shocked to find thousands of cars and trucks. The Iraqi soldiers were going from car to car and stealing everything from the people. When Azza protested and told the Iraqis she had worked hard for her things, they just laughed at her and said, "Consider this a gift to Iraq." She felt furious with them but because she was alone with two children there was little she could do. Her children were yelling at her to lower her voice and not yell at the soldiers. Azza noticed some people trying to bribe the soldiers. They would take the bribe and then steal everything anyway.

Azza knew she was in trouble when she saw the line of cars in front of the Jordanian border patrol. She figured it would take at least two days to get through. By this time she had no food and very little water left, so she drove to the side and begged the guards to let her drive off the road and into the city. Because she was alone with two babies the guards took pity on her and let her pass.

After arriving in Jordan, Azza panicked. Adel had still not shown up and she felt sure the Iraqis had imprisoned him. She was sorry that he had gone back for his brother's car. She felt sorry they had come through Iraq. Walking down the street with her two babies in tow, she suddenly saw Adel walking down the other side of the street. Azza felt light-headed and started screaming with joy. She ran toward Adel with her arms stretched out and he ran toward her and the babies with outstretched arms, as they uttered cries of relief and shed tears of joy.

They made their way to Cairo, where Azza's family helps them to survive while Adel looks for a job. Azza can't forget all she has seen. Many of her memories haunt her and others make her angry. She will never forgive the Iraqis or the Palestinians, who joined the Iraqis despite the kindness the Kuwaitis had shown them. The Palestinians showed Azza their stolen goods. They said the Kuwaitis were never coming back and that Kuwait would belong to them. They called Azza a stupid Egyptian for not joining in the looting.

Azza feels strongly the loss of goods she and Adel worked so hard to buy. But mostly she worries about the handicapped children, without food or anyone to care for them. The law of the jungle has taken over in Kuwait; how can innocent children survive?

Yehina Hamza Ahmed Hamza

If Yehina Hamza lives to be 100 years old, he will never erase the horrors of the war from his mind. Nothing less than the darkness of a tomb will remove the pictures from his memory.

Yehina Hamza is an Egyptian who had lived happily for fifteen years in Kuwait with his wife and six children.

It was Thursday, August 2, at 3:00 A.M. and Yehina was exhausted. As editor of *Al-Nba* and a perfectionist, he had been working all night on the next edition of the paper. Finally satisfied, he went home to catch some sleep.

Just as Yehina was gratefully crawling into bed, he was startled by the ringing of the phone. It was a friend screeching in Yehina's ear that the Iraqis had invaded Kuwait. It took a few moments for the words to sink in. When they did, an astonished Yehina threw on his clothes and drove back to his office.

The newspaper offices were filled with excited employees and Kuwaiti citizens who were running in with shocking stories of Iraqis occupying the middle of the city, the Emir's palace, and all the television and radio stations. Everyone was stunned by the attack. They soon realized that this was a complete takeover of the country.

They heard bombing at the Ministry of Defense, which was very close to the newspaper offices. Looking out the windows, they saw that Iraqi troops and tanks had completely surrounded the Ministry. Yehina and the other staff members watched in stunned disbelief as the drama unfolded.

There were about 300 Kuwaiti soldiers with light arms defending the Ministry. The battle was relatively brief due to the large number of heavily armed Iraqis. After a few hours, finally recognizing defeat and in an attempt to save the lives of their men, the Kuwaiti officers surrendered. Yehina and his staff watched in horror as the Iraqis gathered the weapons and then systematically fired upon the Kuwaitis until they were dead or dying. It only took the Iraqis about fifteen minutes to kill at least 300 men, perhaps more. The murder of all those young men was totally unnecessary; the Iraqis had wanted to show brutality and they succeeded. Over the next six weeks, Yehina saw many unforgettable acts of savagery but nothing compared to the slaughter at the Ministry of Defense. After viewing such a sight, there was little hope for Kuwait or its occupants. With a rush of relief, he thanked God that his wife and six children were in Egypt for the summer.

Speechless, Yehina and his staff wandered back to their offices and faxed out the momentous story of the Iraqi takeover. Their fax lines were still open to Bahrain so the offices were humming with activity. Suddenly, they were inundated by Kuwaiti soldiers relating alarming tales. The Iraqi advance was moving much faster than anyone could have anticipated. The airport had already been taken and the Iraqis were speeding toward the Saudi border. The soldiers were nervous but their morale was high since they felt help would soon come.

The Kuwaiti soldiers were unarmed, although this did not prevent the Iraqi soldiers from methodically shooting any Kuwaiti in uniform. The Kuwaiti soldiers began to strip off their uniforms and request civilian clothes. Yehina's staff rushed about trying to find something for the soldiers to wear. Many of the soldiers fled the offices in their underwear. The employees and Kuwaiti civilians drove some of them to their homes.

Since the Iraqis targeted the TV stations and the radio stations, there was little news reaching the Kuwaiti people. But there was one radio set out in the desert that kept broadcasting through Friday. The voice kept calling for other Arabs to help their Kuwaiti brothers. "Your brothers from Kuwait are calling for your help. Come and help your brothers." The Kuwaitis waited but there was to be no help.

The Iraqis showed their hatred of the Kuwaitis in many ways. They totally destroyed any dwelling that belonged to the ruling family, Al-Sabah. They set up checkpoints and questioned all Kuwaitis who passed; they were looking for certain Kuwaitis who held high positions in the government or whose last name happened to be Al-Sabah. Yehina and his staff helplessly watched from their office windows as the Iraqis pulled these people from their cars. Many times they would shoot the people on the spot, unmindful of their victims' pleas for mercy. Other times they would load the people up and take them to Baghdad, where their fate remains unknown. Yehina saw infants and young children abandoned in cars while their parents were killed or taken away. He and his staff were dazed by too many inhumane sights for any human to absorb.

On the seventh day, the Iraqis came to the newspaper office. The head official met with Yehina and informed him that the newspaper would begin to operate under the orders of the Iraqi government. When Yehina protested that he could not morally justify printing Iraqi propaganda, he was coldly told that he had no choice. He would print what he was told or else. Yehina kept quiet. The Iraqi left, satisfied that he had frightened Yehina into following Iraqi orders.

Yehina then called a meeting of his staff and informed them of the order. His staff unanimously agreed to not cooperate with the enemy. Yehina ordered the destruction of necessary printing equipment. The Iraqis would not be able to utilize the printing presses with or without a trained Kuwaiti staff.

Feeling good about their actions, the staff cautiously left the building in ones and twos and hid in the homes of friends or relatives. They knew the Iraqis would be looking for them. Yehina was the last to leave.

Yehina and his staff held secret meetings while keeping a low profile. They assumed false identities and notified the resistance that they would assist in printing up resistance flyers and leaflets, which proclaimed: "Kuwait for the Kuwaitis," "Bring Back the Emir," "Kuwait, God, and Jaber," and so forth.

For six weeks Yehina stayed in Kuwait, working with his staff and with the resistance. In the beginning, the resistance was an individual effort with many acts of bravery, but after a few weeks it became much more organized and effective. Many Kuwaiti men outside the country at the time of the invasion slipped across the borders and offered their expertise. Other Kuwaiti men took their wives and children to safety in Saudi Arabia and returned to fight. By the sixth week, around 70 to 80 Iraqi soldiers were being killed per night. This toll halted Iraqi looting and raping in Kuwaiti neighborhoods. Unfortunately, the tactic of guerilla warfare caused an unexpected retaliation on the part of the Iraqis. Innocent civilians were made to pay for resistance activity. The Iraqis surrounded a Kuwaiti neighborhood of approximately 40 homes. They forcibly removed all occupants and separated them into groups of men and women. The Kuwaitis were forced to watch the destruction of every home. Afterward, the Iraqis announced to the Kuwaitis that their actions were in answer to the Kuwaiti resistance. Then they took away all the men and left the women and children homeless.

A few days before Yehina slipped out of Kuwait to join his family in Egypt, the Iraqis made an ominous move. They arrested all the young Kuwaiti men between the ages of 16 and 22. Later they took the men up to age 30 and then to age 45. No one knows what happened to many of the young men of Kuwait. The possibilities are too abhorrent to consider.

•

Eaabal Abu-Mustafa

Of all the stories leaking from bleeding Kuwait, none are more heartbreaking than the plight of the sick and injured. As the Iraqi soldiers advanced, they emptied the hospitals and looted the life-saving equipment.

What happened to the Kuwaiti people who depended upon this equipment? Many Kuwaitis fled their country in order to save their lives or those of family members. Others died after being turned back at the border by Iraqi soldiers. The patients who were unconscious never had a fighting chance, for they were unhooked from equipment and taken away to die in some unknown location. It was a terrible stroke of luck to be injured or seriously ill in Kuwait on August 2, 1990.

And what happened to all the babies that were torn from incubators and thrown to die upon the cold floors? Eaabal Abu-Mustafa, a Kuwaiti wife and mother, received a phone call from a doctor friend pleading with her to come to the hospital and take a baby. The doctor had

gathered up the babies from the floor and was
making a heroic effort to find the parents so that
they could come and make some attempt to
save their helpless infants. Tragically, in the
madness of war, he could not locate many of
the parents. Some of the babies did not have on
identification bracelets and the incubators that
listed their names and those of their parents
had been stolen.

Eaabal listened to the doctor's story with
horror. Risking her life, she made her way
across the war-torn city. When she arrived at
the hospital, she was stunned at the number of
sick and injured who were laying unattended
in the hallways. Finally, she found the doctor in
a room full of screaming babies. He was rushing from infant to infant in a vain attempt to
save each tiny life. He thrust a crying baby girl
into Eaabal's arms and told her to take the child
and try to save it. Eaabal looked around the
room in despair. One eighteen-month-old tod-
dler caught her eye. He was moaning piteously.
The doctor explained that he had had surgery
the previous day and it was unlikely he would
survive without medical care. The doctor had
not been able to find any records on the child
nor had the parents shown up to claim their
baby.

Eaabal knew she could not leave without the crying baby boy. She scooped up the child and left the hospital with two babies in her arms, shouting to the doctor to call her if the parents came to claim their children. She returned home to an astonished husband. Hearing the story, the entire family set about to save the two suffering babies.

One week later, the babies were still alive but weakening. Eaabal and her family decided that she would have to chance crossing the desert to Saudi Arabia, where they could receive medical treatment. Otherwise, the family knew they would be forced to watch the unbearable: two innocent babies dying a slow and painful death. Eaabal said good-bye to her family.

Her youngest child, a nine-year-old son, tearfully watched his mother drive away with the two infants. Happily, she arrived safely in Saudi Arabia, and the two babies received the proper treatment to save their young lives.

Although she shudders at the thought of the Kuwaiti parents who are searching in vain for their little ones, Eaabal knows she did the right thing. While the Iraqi ambassador to the United States may declare that all such stories are lies, Eaabal knows just who is lying, for she has two babies who are not her own as verification.

Dr. Yihya Mohamad Ahmad

As was usual, Yihya got up at 6:00 a.m. on the morning of August 2 and dressed for work, unaware of the arrival of Iraqi troops. As he started to get in his car, a neighbor shouted out his bedroom window that there seemed to be some sort of trouble on the border and perhaps Yihya should stay home instead of going to work. Yihya was used to hearing about the Iraqi threats, which had become commonplace the past few weeks, and he shrugged off the warning.

The Al-Jahra Hospital, where Yihya worked as a specialist in anesthesia was located close to the Iraqi-Kuwaiti border. Along the 30-mile drive, Yihya was surprised to see that he was the only car headed toward Iraq. When he spotted a long line of tanks raising red flags toward Kuwait City, he began to wonder about his neighbor's admonition. When he reached his exit, his path was blocked by military jeeps, so he tried another exit. At the second exit, an Iraqi soldier approached his car carrying a machine gun and shouted for Yihya to go back into Kuwait City. Yihya, not yet realizing the seriousness of the situation, argued with the soldier. He told him he was a doctor and he had to get to the hospital. The soldier seemed shocked at Yihya's attitude and let him pass. Yihya was lucky; he later found out that the Iraqi soldiers would shoot anyone who argued with them.

Upon arriving at the hospital, Yihya had no doubt that a war was raging. The Iraqis had already passed through Jahra, and in a matter of hours the hospital had ceased to function. The Asian laundry workers huddled in the basement, refusing to work. The orderlies who transported patients were fleeing the hospital. The Iraqis took the food and the food truck. Patients who were able to move ran down the corridors and out the doors, still in their hospital gowns. Yihya was astounded to see that the hallways were packed with hospital nurses. The raping of Kuwaiti women had already begun, and the women sought refuge together.

By the growing number of injuries, Yihya knew the battle outside must be fierce. Soon he and his colleagues became supermen, performing in an atmosphere they would have considered impossible only the day before. The hospital was filled with the dying and wounded, and many expired before they could be prepared for surgery. There were numerous chest and abdominal injuries. As the only anesthesiologist on duty, Yihya did not leave the operating room once that first day, and he stopped counting the number of surgeries at 100.

The situation became worse after the area was secured, for the Iraqi soldiers took over the hospital. Hundreds of men burst through the doors with drawn weapons. Those patients who had been too sick to flee were ordered to leave. Those unconscious were taken away. One floor was completely emptied and filled with Iraqi doctors, officers, guards, and administrators. The soldiers began to accompany the wounded Iraqis into the emergency and operating rooms. They pointed their weapons at the physicians who treated their Iraqi comrades, threatening death to any doctor who failed to save the life of an Iraqi soldier.

As the Iraqi casualties increased, Iraqi physicians arrived to treat the soldiers' wounds. Yihya was told that the Iraqis had received orders from Baghdad to keep the large number of dead and wounded Iraqis a secret. Saddam Hussein had been shocked by the deadly Kuwaiti resistance and was determined to keep the Iraqi population unaware of the tremendous price they were paying to invade their small neighbor.

Yihya came close to death over the photo of Saddam Hussein. The first day, the Iraqi soldiers had ripped the photos of the Emir and the Crown Prince of Kuwait off the walls and replaced them with the photo of Saddam Hussein. Yihya smiles when he recalls the writings under the photo of Saddam: "Saddam Hussein, Hero of War and Peace and Extraordinary Leader." Yihya and his colleagues tried to ignore the obnoxious photo. Apparently they succeeded, for they did not even notice when the photo was removed by some unknown Kuwaiti patriot. The Iraqis noticed. They rushed into the physicians' lounge and held Yihya and his colleagues at gunpoint, threatening to kill them all if they did not point out the guilty party. Innocent of the knowledge the Iraqis were seeking, the doctors barely managed to convince the soldiers that they were telling the truth. Finally, the Iraqis lowered their guns, but told the doctors in no uncertain terms that they would all die should Hussein's photo be removed again. From that moment the hospital staff tried to keep a close watch on Hussein's

The Saif Palace, built by Mubarak the Great, and used as offices by the Crown Prince. The graffiti says, "We are all Jaber and Saif [the Emir and the Crown Prince]. We are all for Kuwait and we want no one except them."

An Iraqi tank, blown up in the night by Kuwaiti resistance fighters.

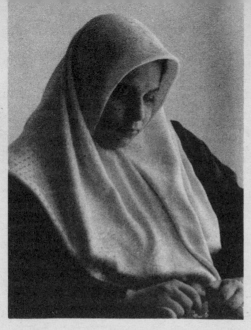

Khalid and Wafa Al-Khayat. *Their family paid a terrible price for the folly of Saddam Hussein.*

Nusaiba and Talal Al-Essa. *The Al-Essa family fled Kuwait in such a hurry that they didn't call any other family members to let them know they were leaving. They feared for the safety of their children.*

Fuad Al-Hashem. *"I hope one day I get to see that Iraqi soldier that stole my car! I want to thank him! He saved my life...."*

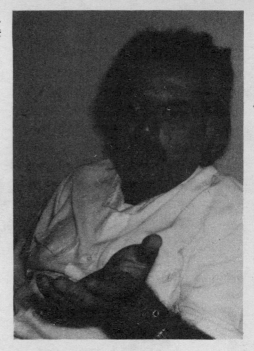

Azza Salah Abd Eimotlai. *"An enemy from the outside attacked Kuwait, and then a silent enemy, the Palestinians, attacked from within."*

Yehina Hamza Ahmed Hamza. *"The newspaper staff was horrified to witness the Iraqis surround and kill over 300 Kuwaiti soldiers at the Ministry of Defense. The Kuwaitis had surrendered. They were slaughtered."*

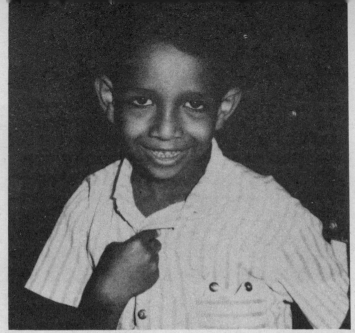

REFUGEES, KUWAITI EMBASSY IN CAIRO, EGYPT

An eight-year-old boy smiles for the camera. He dreams of going home soon, so that he won't miss too many days of school.

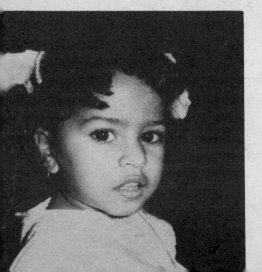

Only three years old, Basma Sulaiman is too young to understand the implications of the changes in her life. Two weeks after the invasion, she escaped with her mother through Iraq. Basma spends her days at the embassy in Cairo with her mother, fearfully awaiting word of loved ones trapped in Kuwait.

Disbelieving of the tragedy that overtook their lives, Kuwaiti men silently search a bulletin board at the embassy in Cairo for news of their missing family members.

Mohamad Al Mijrin Al Roumi, *a counselor at the embassy in Cairo, spends his days and often much of his nights attempting to solve the individual problems of his citizens.*

Ahmad Khattab Al-Othman, *a 70-year-old grand-father, with the author and Balkees. He was taken to Cairo in July for medical care. When the invasion occurred, he was the only member of his family outside the country. He journeys daily to the embassy in Cairo to try to find news of his children and grandchildren. He is completely alone.*

Balkees worked tirelessly with the author in Cairo locating Kuwaitis and Egyptians who had escaped the cruel Iraqi occupation.

Abdulla Al-Ali *left Kuwait six weeks after the invasion. He witnessed the brutal killing of one of his employees at the hands of the Iraqi troops. His four brothers are missing; his sister suffers from breast cancer and cannot find the necessary medication.*

Rabia al-Sarre *drove across the border with her sisters. "The Saudi border guards told me that I could not drive into Saudi Arabia. Since I was the only person in the car that could drive, I asked them, do you want me to go back?"*

REFUGEES, KUWAIT EMBASSY IN RIYADH, SAUDI ARABIA

Stranded Kuwaiti men gather at the gates of their embassy in Riyadh to seek information about their families and their country.

Dr. Yihya Mohamad Ahmad. *"The first day I was unable to leave the Operating Theatre. We treated over 100 cases of gunshot wounds."*

"Nizad," resistance fighter. His real name is withheld to protect his identity.

Nadia Al-Hosney. *"Saddam Hussein killed our dream when he invaded Kuwait. Our dream of Arab unity."*

This beautiful Kuwaiti woman housed in the school feels compelled to cover her face for photos, since her husband is still trapped inside Kuwait. Many Kuwaitis fear their relatives will be punished for an appearance in this book.

A six-year-old at the housing project proudly pointed out a photo of the Emir. He had carried the photo with him across the desert and displayed it on the wall of the school room. Many young children were shot and killed by the Iraqis for possessing this same photo.

Children at a school housing project in Riyadh

The people and government of Saudi Arabia opened their hearts and their homes to the Kuwaiti refugees that escaped the cruel occupation of their homeland. After the hotels, apartments, and private homes overflowed, the Saudi government opened the doors of the schools and delayed the school year for their own children.

Thankful for a shelter while waiting to return home, Kuwaiti families crowd into small classrooms and try to bring some order to their lives. The men are housed on one floor, the women and children on another floor.

These small children, delighted at the opportunity to voice their opinions, gleefully make victory signs and chant for President Bush to go to their country and to flog and jail the evil man, Saddam Hussein.

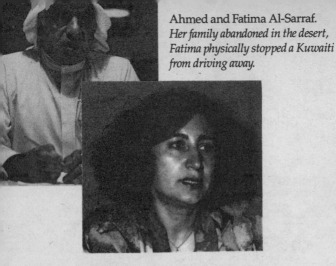

Ahmed and Fatima Al-Sarraf.
*Her family abandoned in the desert,
Fatima physically stopped a Kuwaiti
from driving away.*

Nora Abd-Allah. *"I was not
afraid of the Iraqis. I answer
only to God, not to Iraqis.
Besides, a person can only
die once."*

Sara Al-Fahad. *"Kuwait was
like a nightmare come true."*

Sheik Fahd Ahmed Al-Jabir Al-Sabah. *Fahd could have fled the invading army, but the thought never entered his mind. Instead, he ran toward the Iraqis. He was killed the first day of the invasion by Iraqi soldiers while he was defending the Dasman Palace, the home of his brother, the Emir.*

Dr. Souad Abdullah Al-Sabah, *a renowned Arab poet and writer. Since the invasion of her country by Saddam Hussein, she has produced a flood of articles and poems condemning his action.*

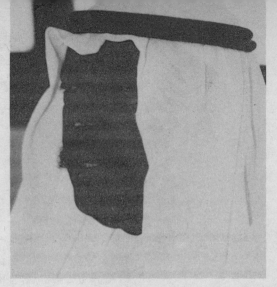

His Highness Sheik Saad Al-Abdallah Al-Salem
Al-Sabah, Crown Prince and Prime Minister

Sheik Jaber Al-Ahmad
Al-Sabah, The Emir of
Kuwait

photo; they knew the Iraqis would keep their word.

Yihya was in the ICU when five young children between ages four and ten were brought in. They had been marching in a peaceful demonstration when the Iraqis opened fire. The children were bleeding heavily. Their parents were crying in anguish. Despite the doctors' frantic efforts, only two could be saved. Yihya and the other physicians asked each other, What kind of a man can shoot a four-year-old child?

The nurses' worst fears came true. In the beginning of the battle there had been random rapes. This continued threat haunted the women of the hospital, and they begged the Iraqis to let them leave the area and travel out of Kuwait. The Iraqis refused. Instead, they forced the nurses to go back to their living quarters and then they surrounded their apartments with guards. The Iraqis turned the apartments of the nurses into a brothel. At night, the soldiers would enter the buildings and force the women to stand in a line. Then they would pick and choose. If a woman resisted, she was beaten severely with a rifle butt. The soldiers were brutal with the women and left them in shock, with painful cuts and bruises. The youngest and most attractive of the nurses were raped repeatedly by large numbers of soldiers. Three in particular, two Egyptian and one Indian nurse, were the favorites of the soldiers. Raped continuously, they were suffering from shock and barely able to speak when the physicians treated their wounds. Unable to escape, the women could only sit and wait for their next attacker.

By September 7, Yihya felt he could no longer function as a physician under Iraq's cruel occupation. He had no medications, the hospital had virtually stopped treating civilians, and the Iraqis threatened his life on a daily basis. He made his dash for freedom through Iraq and Jordan. The city had become a world gone mad.

Nizar

If Nizar had thought for one moment that Saddam Hussein was going to send his armies into Kuwait, he would never have gone to Egypt in July. Instead, he would have been alongside his two brothers that died defending their country on the morning of August 2. The moment he heard the news, he got on a plane and flew to Saudi Arabia. From there he crossed the border into Kuwait. Disbelieving of the stories of destruction inside Kuwait, he went to look for himself. He had to see his country and nothing could have stopped him.

Nizar belongs to a line of men who are willing to die for their country, and he has been in a fighting mood since the day he saw what the Iraqis were doing to his land and his people.

A leader in the resistance, Nizar has crossed the border six times since he first went back into the country. He had intentions to go back and forth across the desert but there were desperate women and children inside Kuwait who needed help escaping. Nizar took it upon himself to try and save as many of them as possible. He delivered human cargo to safety in Saudi Arabia and on his return trip carried in guns and supplies for the resistance. The journey was far from secure and easy, as Iraqis had orders to fire on vehicles in the desert. Nizar has been shot and he has lost one passenger. He tries to think of the large number of women and children he has saved and not dwell on his sorrow when remembering the teenage girl that was shot and killed by the Iraqis.

Nizar was making a run across the border when out of nowhere Iraqi soldiers appeared and started emptying their guns at his vehicle. Knowing that he and his passengers would be slaughtered if he stopped, Nizar hit the gas pedal and outran the bullets. He didn't stop until he arrived at the Saudi border. Everyone was excited and thanking God that they were safe when Nizar noticed one of the teenage girls had her head back on the seat and was not talking. He felt his heart stop when he called her name and she did not respond. With a sense of foreboding, he got everyone out of the car and lifted her head. There was a clean shot that had entered her head and had lodged inside. The girl was dead. Nizar wanted to deliver women and children to Saudi Arabia alive, not dead.

Nizar himself was shot while driving a group of ten women and children across the desert. Just when he was thanking God for keeping him out of sight of the Iraqis, he felt a terrible pain in his side and chest. Convinced that the stress of the war and the fighting was giving him a heart attack he vowed to himself to stay calm and not let his passengers know that their driver might collapse at any moment. He had to hang on long enough to make the Saudi border. Then he would have his heart attack. The pain became so severe that he was afraid he would pass out, so he pressed the left side of his chest with his right hand in an attempt to ease his discomfort. Shocked to feel his hand wet, he pulled it to his face and saw blood. Realizing he had been shot and not wanting to alarm the women and children, he held his chest tight until he arrived in Saudi Arabia. Examined by a doctor, he was declared lucky that the bullet had entered the fleshy part of his body and failed to hit any vital organs. Nizar is still baffled as to the location of the Iraqi who shot him.

Several weeks before he was shot, Nizar was rounded up by Iraqi security and questioned. The Iraqis had just started their program of interrogating Kuwaiti men and they happened to snare Nizar as he was walking the streets of Kuwait City. Traveling with false papers, Nizar hoped his true identity was not known. If so, he knew he was in real trouble. The Iraqis first asked him for the names of resistance members. When Nizar told them he had no knowledge of the resistance, they started beating him. Then they applied electrical shocks to his nipples and his genitals. Nizar stuck to his same story for two days of torture. Finally, the Iraqis decided that he really did not know anything and he was released. Nizar smiles when he thinks how stupid the Iraqis were to let him get away. They had a leader of the resistance and just let him go.

Nizar talked to some other Iraqi soldiers, pretending to be friendly to them in order to collect all possible information. He wandered up to an Iraqi on a tank, and started a friendly conversation. The Iraqi felt at ease and asked Nizar if he could give him some information. Nizar eased closer. The Iraqi leaned toward Nizar and whispered: "Tell me, who is this man called Bush?" Nizar filled him in on world events. Then the soldier said, "When is this Bush coming?" Nizar replied, "Soon." The soldier nodded and continued, "Look what I have," as he pointed under his seat. He had a white cloth, folded up and ready to surrender. The Iraqi soldier laughed and said, "When this Bush man comes, I am ready. I will wave my arms in the air and then go to America."

Eager to return to Kuwait, Nizar is a man possessed. He has lost two brothers to Saddam Hussein and two others are missing.

Well-known and famous with his people, Nizar recognizes that no matter how hard he and others like him fight, they will never get the Iraqis out of Kuwait without help. "We are a small country but we are willing to fight. Let us walk first into the battle, into Saddam's bullets. We will die. But someone will have to come behind us to take the land. We accept the bullets. We accept death. Help us, please"

A Kuwaiti resistance fighter, Nizar's real name has been withheld to protect his identity.

The Rape of Three Women:
A Crime Never Forgiven
or Forgotten

Many stories have come out of Kuwait about the rape of young women and girls, sometimes in front of their parents, by the Iraqi soldiers. This outrage, so incomprehensible to the Kuwaitis, was responsible for the high number of Kuwaiti refugees. Rape is not a common occurrence in most Middle Eastern conflicts, since it is punishable by the death not only of the rapist but of his entire family as well. Indeed, for all the lawlessness in Lebanon during the past 15 years (since the start of the civil war in 1975), the crime of rape has been a rare occurrence. It was, therefore, difficult to arrange interviews with women refugees who were raped by the invading Iraqi soldiers. The horrors of the crime as witnessed by these women were particularly tragic, for rape is not acceptable in Middle Eastern societies. Therefore, it took tremendous courage for these women to come forth and tell their stories. Nevertheless, I have changed the names of the three women whose stories follow, to protect their privacy and, if possible, lessen their shame.

Haifa Al-Rumaihi

Haifa Al-Rumaihi doesn't care what other Kuwaitis say, she will hate all Iraqis until the day she dies. She is bitter and shivers in anger when she says the word "Iraqi". She used to have Iraqi friends, but never again. She hopes the army of Saudi Arabia drops nuclear bombs on the country and kills every Iraqi. Haifa's anger keeps her sane. On August 4, two days after the invasion, Haifa and her husband, Mohammed, decided to leave Kuwait, so fearful were they for the safety of their two young children. On Saturday, August 4, Mohammed left the house in order to go and collect enough gas to make the journey across the desert into Saudi Arabia leaving Haifa alone in the apartment with the children. Suddenly Haifa heard loud voices at the door. She hid her two babies in her bedroom closet. Her five month old was asleep but her two year old was whimpering when she closed the door.

She knew it was the Iraqis when she heard their accents. She shouted through the door and asked them what they wanted. They told her to open up or they would shoot through the door.

Haifa thought they sounded drunk and refused to open the door. She ran into the dining room and grabbed a knife. She thought the soldiers might try and harm her babies. Her heart stopped as they kicked in the door.

There were three of them and they were intoxicated. They asked her if her husband was home. One of them pointed his gun at her and told Haifa that if she didn't put down the knife he would shoot. Haifa put down the knife and begged the soldiers to leave. She knew that if Mohammed returned there would be a terrible situation.

The soldiers went to the refrigerator and took out some chicken and hummus. They cursed when they didn't find any alcohol. Sitting down to eat, they told Haifa not to move. After eating, the soldiers sat and picked their teeth. One of them stood up and horrified Haifa by asking her to show him to the bedroom. She pointed in the direction of the spare room. Her main concern was to keep them away from the children in the master bedroom. The soldier then grabbed her arm and said, "No, don't point. Show me the bedroom. The one with the biggest bed." The other two soldiers started to laugh and they all three pushed her into the bedroom.

Haifa appealed to their belief in God and told them that what they were planning was against God's teachings. Desperate, she asked them if they had sisters or mothers and what would they do if someone attacked the women of their families. None of her pleas moved them. While they were pushing down the hallway, her two-year-old daughter came screaming toward Haifa. One of the soldiers grabbed the crying child and held a gun to her head. He told Haifa that if she didn't show them a good time, her baby would receive a bullet in her head. The soldier pushed the front of the gun into her baby's ear. Haifa became hysterical and told the soldiers she would do anything, but not to shoot her baby.

The soldiers stayed with Haifa for over two hours. The baby sat in the corner and cried the entire time. Haifa can't think about what shameful things the soldiers forced her to do, much less talk about it. She can't even tell her husband, although he has been loving and supportive since he came home and found her naked and crying in the corner of the spare room. She was holding their sobbing baby daughter.

Haifa feels dirty no matter how many baths she takes. She cries a lot. Her husband wants to go with her to counseling but Haifa is too ashamed. She is afraid the counselor will ask specific questions andHaifa says she can never tell anyone exactly what happened to her in those two hours.Her shame is unbearable.

Cora Pelaez

On January 4, 1990, Cora Pelaez travelled to Kuwait from Manila with hope in her heart. Cora's father had died when she was only seven and from that moment, life had been a continuous struggle for the family. Cora had watched her mother, who had five young children to clothe and feed, grow old quickly as she worked in the fields just to put a little rice on the table.

Their lot had improved slightly when Cora's older brother managed to get a job as a driver in Dubai in 1988. He sent $150.00 to them each month and, for the first time in their lives, there was meat on the table at least once every week. They celebrated for a week when her mother purchased two buffaloes and three pigs in the summer of 1989 and were well on their way to prosperity when in August, 1989, they learned that Cora's brother had been killed in a car accident in Dubai. Cora's mother didn't even have the money to bring her eldest son's body back to the Philippines but a rich Arab had taken pity on them when he read the story in the newspaper and he had paid all the expenses.

Now the oldest living child, Cora went to an agency in Manila and put in her application as a maid for any of the Arab states. The agency told her there wasn't much hope, since they had 500 applicants for every job opening, but they would keep her in mind.

In November, Cora's mother discovered a lump in her breast. It was as big as a golf ball and the doctor told Cora's mother that it had probably already spread and she would need surgery and chemotherapy. When Cora's mother told him she had no money, the doctor told her to prepare to die.

Cora went back to Manila and begged the agency to get her a job, any job, so that she could pay for her mother's surgery. She knew if she got a job in one of the rich Arab countries, the doctor would do the surgery and let her pay a little each month. The man at the agency was Lebanese and he took pity on her. He scratched off a name on a list and put Cora's name in its place. He told her to leave her passport and to come back in ten days prepared to go to Kuwait. She had a job.

Cora's mother had surgery two days before Cora left for Kuwait. The cancer had spread and the doctor warned that chemotherapy might not save her life. Cora owed him $5,000.00 and she had to pay him back $200.00 a month until it was paid off. The doctor charged her 20% interest. Cora knew she was only making $300.00 a month but she planned to stay in Kuwait a long time. She would pay the doctor $200.00 and send her mother $100.00. Cora didn't need any money since her employers would give her food.

Cora cried when she got on the plane for Kuwait but it was because she was so happy. She felt like she had saved her mother's life. She bowed her head and thanked God. She promised herself that she was going to work so hard that her employers would give her a small raise each year. After all, her younger sister was smart and would need money for college in a few years.

Cora's employers lived in a town called Jahra in Kuwait. The lady of the house had a really sweet nature and she smiled at Cora's eager efforts to please. Her husband was always soft-spoken and never mistreated her in any way. Cora was happy to be with a kind family. On the twenty-eighth of each month, she would send money to the Philippines, and sing for days afterward, thinking of the excitement when the money was delivered to the little hut in the village. She imagined her mother walking to the meat market and selecting various pieces of meat for the stew she would prepare weekly. She even thought of the family sitting around the small table enjoying the food that Cora was putting on the table.

In July, Cora's employers left for their annual holiday in France. The house seemed so big and empty with only four people left. The Indian yardman wasn't much company. He was constantly plotting ways to go to the Souk area and meet his Sri Lankan girlfriend. The cook was from Pakistan and she cried all the time from missing her children. That left Cora and the other maid who was also from the Philippines, but she was much older than Cora and barely talked to her. The Indian yardman said it was because Cora was so pretty and the other maid was jealous because she was nothing but a fat cow. He winked at Cora when he said it and Cora avoided him from then on. Cora had never had a date or even thought about a boyfriend. Her life had been spent trying to find enough food to eat. The people in her village had told her she was pretty but she had never owned a mirror and had barely glanced at herself in the shops when she went into the village. She was always so embarrassed at the rags she had to wear that she thought if she did not see herself that no one else would either.

Toward the end of July the Indian yardman told Cora that Saddam Hussein, the president of Iraq, had massed troops on the border and that he was mad at the Kuwaitis about oil and money. When the yardman saw her concerned look, he squeezed her arm and told her not to worry, that the Arabs were always arguing about something and it usually didn't amount to much of anything. But Cora felt otherwise. She started watching the news and asking the other Filipino maid to translate the Arabic for her. The other maid had lived in Kuwait for eight years and understood the language.

Since their bosses were out of the country, Cora and the other employees slept late. On August 2, Cora was laying on her back, staring up at the ceiling when she heard thumping noises. She couldn't figure out what it was but she didn't want to get up so she closed her eyes and daydreamed about her mother and her younger sisters and brothers. Since she only got one month's holiday every two years, she wouldn't see them for another year and a half, but Cora derived a lot of pleasure thinking of the small gifts she would take home and what they all would talk about.

Cora drifted back to sleep but a loud bang awakened her around 9:00 A.M. She heard screaming and shouting. She jumped to her feet and grabbed her blue cotton robe.

Cora screamed when she saw the Indian yardman laying in a pool of blood at the front door. She saw soldiers with guns but she didn't know where they had come from. The Pakistani cook ran past her and yelled that it was the Iraqis. She shouted for Cora to run out the back door. Cora stood paralyzed with fear. She tried to make her feet move toward the door but she couldn't move. She shook her head and started crying when the Iraqis came toward her. They were laughing and speaking loud in Arabic but she didn't know what they were saying. She thought they were going to shoot her too and all she could think about was her family in the Philippines. How would they survive?

Cora was confused when the soldiers started pushing her back and tugging at her robe. When she realized what they were going to do, she began to fight like a tiger. She didn't stand a chance. She was too small and there were too many of them, perhaps six. Within seconds,

Cora was naked and down on the floor. The soldiers put down their guns and four of them held her arms and legs while a fifth raped her. Cora screamed so loudly that the soldiers took her gown and gagged her. It seemed to make them angry that she was a virgin and bled a lot. All of the soldiers raped her and three of them raped her twice. They raped her in every possible place and way.

Cora thought that the soldiers were never going to stop. Finally, after she had fainted, they left. When she awakened, she heard the yardman groaning. As Cora looked at him across the room, she saw bubbles of blood coming out of his mouth and his whole body shuddered. After that, he didn't move anymore. Cora crawled slowly across the room and looked at him. She knew he was dead. Terrified that the soldiers would return, she crawled out into the garden and hid behind some bushes. She stayed there until the next day. She knew she needed medical attention but didn't know what to do or where to go. Finally, she forced herself to go into the house and get into a tub of water. The bleeding started up again when she got into a hot bath and she thought she was going to bleed to death. Finally she remembered her mother saying that cold water would stop bleeding. She filled the tub with cold water and dumped ice cubes inside and made herself sit in it until the bleeding stopped. It was in the tub that Cora noticed that her left nipple was gone. She had felt stinging pain in her breast and the blood running onto her stomach. Her lower stomach and rectum hurt her so badly that she had not even noticed that someone had bitten off her left nipple. She made a bandage of sorts and looked for pain medication but couldn't find anything but baby aspirin. She took that, but it didn't seem to ease the pain.

Cora knew that she had to get out of Kuwait. She ate some food and painfully dressed in a smock. She stepped over the yardman and peeked out the front door. The streets were quiet. Cora went from house to house until she found some other Filipinos. The Filipino women were incensed when they saw Cora's condition. One of them had also been raped but had not suffered such injuries. The Filipino men cursed the Iraqis.

Fortunately, the Filipinos Cora had located were planning an escape to Jordan. Cora felt a rush of relief when she heard their plans, for all she wanted to do was to get back home and see her mother.

The journey through Iraq was hell. They were robbed by Iraqi civilians and had only a few apples and a small amount of water for the entire trip. The Filipinos took care of Cora and comforted her the entire way. Fortunately, one of them was a nurse and doctored Cora's wounds. However, the fourth day, Cora got a bad infection in her breast and pus came out. The pain was indescribable. When they finally got to Jordan, the officials took one look at her and made her one of the first to be evacuated.

Cora will never forget her mother's face when they were finally reunited. Although relieved to see that Cora was alive, Cora's mother was devastated by her condition. Cora told her family that the Iraqis beat her up. She cannot bear to tell them that she was raped. It is a pain that she cannot pass on. She is careful to turn her back when she dresses for she knows her nippleless breast will reveal her dark secret.

Cora has the same nightmare every night. One man with multiple arms is holding her down. He doesn't rape her, he just pins her to the ground with his six hands. He tells her that her family is starving in the Philippines and he is going to hold her down until each of them is dead. When Cora looks at the gaunt faces of her family around her, she feels the reality is worse than any nightmare.

Tahani Salah.

Tahani Salah has made a pledge: One day she will find the Iraqi soldier who raped her and kill him. She has no brother to take revenge and her father is too old. So Tahani will do it herself. She sits by the hour, plotting.

Five years ago, when Tahani was 17, she met an especially nice Kuwaiti girl at school in Cairo, Egypt. Tahani is Egyptian and she befriended the Kuwaiti girl and took her to her home for a visit. Over the years, their friendship developed and even after they finished school at age 20, they made a special point to see each other at least once a year. They made a pact, each year one would travel to the other's home.

This year, it was Tahani's turn to go to Kuwait. However, Tahani's father was concerned about the Iraqi build-up and asked Tahani to phone her friend and postpone the visit, or to ask her friend to come to Cairo. Tahani argued with her father until he finally shrugged his shoulders and gave in. Still, he told her he was worried the day she boarded the Egypt Air flight to Kuwait City on July 22, 1990.

Tahani was groggy with sleep when her father called her in the early hours of the morning of August 2 and told her to get out of Kuwait immediately. But Tahani couldn't believe that she was in personal danger. After all, she was a woman and generally women are not targeted. Still, she wanted to go home as quickly as possible.

The father of Tahani's friend made them stay home the first week after the invasion. He thought that some solution would be reached and that the Iraqis would go back to Iraq. He said that if they waited the crisis out at home, time would take care of the problem. He tried to frighten them by pointing out that they were too pretty and that the Iraqis had been attacking pretty women, but Tahani just couldn't believe the Iraqis were attacking fellow Moslems. Certainly they wouldn't attack Moslem women!

By the eighth day following the invasion, Tahani and her friend were gong crazy. They had not been out of the house and they couldn't stand it another minute. When her friend's father went out that morning around 10:00, they thought they would slip out just to check on the city. They couldn't believe all the reports they had been hearing about the destruction, and wanted to see for themselves. They decided to drive down to the local co-op (supermarket) and see if they could find some ice cream for the children in the house.

The trip to the co-op went smoothly. Although they didn't find any ice cream, they did get some cookies. Feeling adventurous, the girls took the long way home. They weren't afraid when they saw the Iraqi soldiers at a roadblock. Iraqi soldiers were swarming all over Kuwait and so far none had even given them a glance.

Tahani doesn't know why the soldier picked her. She thinks her friend is much prettier. For whatever the reason, the Iraqi soldier who checked their papers at the roadblock told Tahani to get out of the car. He told her friend to leave. Tahani's friend refused to drive off and the Iraqi shot out the back window and tail-lights. He pointed the gun at Tahani's friend and forced her to drive away.

Tahani's whole body went numb when the Iraqi soldier told his buddy to take over the roadblock. He pulled Tahani around to the back of a building and took off her clothes. Tahani didn't make a sound as he raped her because the soldier held his pocket knife to her left eye and said he would pluck out her eye if she screamed or brought attention to them.

After the soldier raped her, he sat back and had two cigarettes. He asked Tahani where she was staying, that he would come and look her up. He wouldn't let Tahani redress and after he put out his cigarette, he raped her again. This time he didn't hold the knife to her eye and when she started to cry, he hit her hard on the ear with his fist. He told her if she didn't stop crying that he would go and get his buddies and they would all have a turn.

Finally the soldier left. Tahani got dressed as quickly as possible and ran crying to the home of her friend.

Three weeks later Tahani managed to cross the border into Saudi Arabia. She flew back to Egypt. When her elderly father heard about the rape, he collapsed and had to be hospitalized. Luckily, he survived, but one day Tahani heard him crying. She had never heard her father cry. At that moment, she knew she had to hunt up that Iraqi and kill him in order to avenge their family name. She has his face memorized and she heard one of the other soldiers call his name as he led her to the back of the building.

Tahani feels her life is ruined, as no Moslem man will want to marry a woman who is not a virgin. Besides, after her experience, she doesn't think she will be a good wife. She hates all men now, except for her father of course. And it is for her father that she is determined to kill the Iraqi rapist. It is her passion for his death that keeps her going.

Nadia Al-Hosney

Nadia's[*] babies were safe. She had just received a phone call from Saudi Arabia informing her that her babies and her mother-in-law had crossed the border safely. She breathed a huge sigh of relief.

Nadia and her husband, Mansoor, were leaders in the Kuwaiti resistance movement since the beginning, and they had no illusions about the severity of the punishment if discovered. Feeling encumbered by the necessity to protect their four little ones, they had been less effective in their resistance work. Recognizing that their fears for their children were affecting their capabilities, Nadia and Mansoor made the painful decision to send them across the border into Saudi Arabia. They knew the trip through the desert would be an enormous risk but they felt that occupied Kuwait would become more violent as the days passed. And there was never

---

[*]Nadia's real name is withheld to protect the identity of her family.

a question in their minds of cooperating with the enemy. They opted for the danger of the desert.

Nadia felt her heart would break as she watched her children being driven away. Her emotions ranged from great hope to darkest terror. The long hours that she knew her babies were in acute danger were the hardest of her life. Any mother would understand the agony. But now she knew she had made the correct choice. Her babies were safe.

From the very beginning Nadia and Mansoor had worked with other Kuwaitis to help their besieged countrymen. Immediately after the invasion they had called a neighborhood meeting and organized themselves. The country had been emptied of fleeing medical personnel, so they worked in the hospitals and assisted the beleaguered medical staff. There was no provision to assist the orphanages, so they carried food to the children. The service sector of the country had ground to a halt, so they emptied the garbage and helped to bake bread. No task seemed too small or too large.

All Kuwaitis had been angry and sickened when they heard Hussein's false claim that the people of Kuwait had asked for Iraqi assistance in overthrowing the corrupt Al-Sabah regime.

While it was true that 30,000 Kuwaitis had petitioned for a reinstatement of the Parliament, there had been no talk of overthrowing the government. The Parliament had been dismantled in 1986 due to political upheaval later associated with Iranian radicals. With the Iranian/Iraqi war behind them, some Kuwaitis thought it was time to reinstate the Parliament. The Kuwaitis handled their problems in peaceable ways. Petitions were the style of their land. Meaty-looking men handling guns did not go over well in Kuwait. With defiant pride all Kuwaitis ignored Saddam Hussein's call for them to step forward and form a new government. They laughed when Saddam could not find one Kuwaiti out of 826,586 citizens to head his puppet government.

As the days passed, there was talk in the neighborhood. Everyone wanted to do even more than they were doing to further the cause of Kuwaiti independence. A decision was made to start a political movement inside the country along with the current civilian and military rebellion. It was decided that the women and children would hold peaceful marches. There was hope that the Iraqis would not fire on children.

Without thought of personal danger, Nadia marched with the women and the children. She carried a sign which read: "Kuwait for the Kuwaitis." Other signs read: "God, Kuwait, and the Emir." Nadia knew the purpose of their march. All Kuwaitis were together on this point, without dissension. These women wanted the world to know that the Kuwaitis did not ask for Iraqi intervention in their country. They did not want these men in their country. They walked slowly and purposely in order to avoid confrontation with the armed soldiers. The march progressed without incident. A son of one of Nadia's friends went unnoticed as he videotaped the march for the resistance. Later, the tape would cross the border and be sent to the West. In a peaceful way, a way they thought would be of little danger to the children, the women and children of Kuwait were doing their part.

The men's tasks were more deadly. At night they patrolled the neighborhoods. They set up ambushes and killed Iraqi soldiers. They stole guns and they destroyed tanks. They frightened the Iraqis and kept them from Kuwaiti homes. And, the Kuwaiti men died. As the violence increased between Iraqis and Kuwaitis, the men became concerned for their women and children. The resistance was successful. It had unnerved the enemy. Now, they knew it would not be long before the Iraqis struck back. The Iraqis had made no attempt to attack the armed men of the resistance but they just might strike at the women or the children.

Nadia cannot recall why she was not marching in the demonstration of September 11. Perhaps some other duty had her attention on that day.

The women and children gathered and moved cautiously down the street. They carried the usual signs and Kuwaiti flags. They were peaceful. They looked straight ahead. They chanted. They made no threatening moves toward the soldiers. They were unarmed.

Suddenly, Iraqis swarmed around the women. They opened fire and shot at their legs. One woman was killed. Others were seriously injured.

Nadia's friend lost her 21-year-old son that day. While videotaping the march, he was surrounded by Iraqis and led away. He cannot be found.

After the attack on the demonstration, many husbands wanted their wives and children out of the country. While willing to risk their own lives, they did not want to witness the deaths of their loved ones. Mansoor wanted Nadia to leave. He told her that she was his weak point. He did not feel free to risk her life. She was the mother of his four daughters. The children would need one parent. He insisted she go to Saudi Arabia and join their babies. Nadia could not bear to leave him but she eventually faced the unbearable. It was the second hardest act of her life.

Nadia carried on her volunteer work in Riyadh. There were many Kuwaiti refugees that needed help. While it was physically safer, she pursued each task as if it were life or death. Her diligence became well-known. She did what she could. And, she waited in vain for some word of Mansoor.

Nadia's eldest daughter confessed pride of her warrior father. She knew her father could never accept waiting outside his country's borders while men of another land claimed Kuwait as their own.

As if she didn't have enough worries, Nadia frets about the Palestinians under Israeli control. She and Mansoor financially supported three Palestinian families. They sent them money for food, rent, and their children's educations. When the Iraqis invaded Kuwait, Nadia and Mansoor lost all their money. As a result, three families in Palestine are without food. Nadia is frantic with worry. In one family, the father is elderly and cannot work. The sons of two of the families are in Israeli prisons and do not have any support. Nadia knows the families will go hungry and the children will have to drop out of school. The repercussions of the Iraqi invasion are felt in the stomachs of Palestinians on the West Bank and in the Gaza Strip.

Nora Al-Gami

The last time Nora Al-Gami spoke with her cousin Hala she was extremely excited. Hala was packing for a trip from Kuwait City to Saudi Arabia to attend a wedding. Pregnant with her fourth child, she was eager for a small outing. Her husband and three young daughters would be accompanying her.

The date was August 1, 1990, and tragedy struck along the way. A speeding tanker ran over the car carrying Hala and her family. When the wreckage was pulled apart, Hala and her 12-month-old baby were pulled dead from the car. Hala's husband, Ali, was severely injured and remained unconscious in the fast-moving ambulance to the Gahra Hospital in Kuwait. Hala's ten-year-old daughter, Yasmine, was screaming in agony from a broken neck and other broken bones. She was also taken to the Gahra Hospital. The middle daughter, Nuda, managed to escape with cuts and bruises and her mother's family took her back to their home in Kuwait.

The following morning, Nora's family was in complete shock over the death of two family members and the doubtful health of two others. They simply could not absorb more bad news when they were hit with the Iraqi invasion of their country. As the enemy swept through Kuwait, they received an early morning phone call from the administrator at the Gahra Hospital advising them to come and get Ali and Yasmine. He told them that the Iraqis were throwing people from their beds. He urged them to hurry!

The family rushed to the Gahra Hospital to rescue their loved ones. They were stunned and disbelieving when they arrived at Ali's bed to find it empty. He had been in intensive care. The tubes were still hanging by his bed. The hospital nurses tearfully told them that the Iraqis had yanked the tubes from Ali's nose and arms and had taken him away. They had taken all the patients from the intensive care unit. Immediately, the family ran down the long corridors to try and find Yasmine. Thankfully, she was located but she had been thrown to the floor and was in terrible pain since she had a broken neck. They felt a rush of relief that she was not dead or at least paralyzed from such treatment. The family lifted her and tried to carry her to the car as gently as possible. Already, the stretchers were missing from the hospital.

The men of the family made tremendous efforts to locate Ali. They were told by other Kuwaitis that the Iraqis had taken a lot of unconscious hospital patients to the skating rink. They had stacked bodies one on top of the other. The men went to the skating rink. They saw many dead and dying but they were not able to find Ali. He was never found.

Meanwhile, Yasmine was in pathetic condition. She was stricken with severe pain and had difficulty breathing. She was taken from one hospital to the other but Kuwaitis were not allowed in the hospitals. The Iraqis pushed them away from the doors and threatened them with their guns. Finally, in view of Yasmine's deteriorating situation, the family decided to take the desert route to Saudi Arabia.

The family left Kuwait in three cars. Hala's sister took responsibility for her dead sister's children. She sat in the back seat with Yasmine while her husband and Nada sat in the front. They were in the third car.

The ride was so bumpy that the family members feared for Yasmine. They wondered how she would ever survive the trip. Their problems intensified at the desert. Spotted by Iraqi soldiers, they were forced to stop. The soldiers robbed the families of everything they had packed and took what little money they had. Then, for some strange reason, the soldiers allowed the first two cars to continue but stopped the third car with the injured Yasmine. When the family members protested and tried to explain Yasmine's condition, the soldiers became angry, pointing their guns in the air, firing them, then pointing them at the cars. They refused to allow the two lead cars to return to Kuwait or to allow the third car to proceed.

Nora weeps when she thinks of the child. She remembers how Yasmine was crying and gasping for breath as she was loaded for the trip. Her neck was so swollen that she had difficulty breathing. Along the road to the border the cars had to stop so that Yasmine could be relieved from the shock of the bumpy roads. Nora will never forget the screams of Yasmine.

◆

Sara Al-Fahad

Sara had to leave Kuwait. Her husband was one of the Kuwaitis who helped foreigners trapped in Kuwait, making sure they had food and keeping them up-to-date on events. He made himself responsible for their safety. And he was being hunted by the Iraqis. If they found him, he would be executed. Sara's children were in danger as well. The Iraqis were questioning young children about their parents' activities, and it was only a matter of time before one of Sara's young sons accidentally revealed the truth: his daddy knew a lot of foreigners and even sheltered some in their home.

Before Sara left, one of her friends died for lack of medical treatment. He was only 36 and he knew he would die without dialysis. He made out his will and then attempted to cross the desert. Caught and returned to Kuwait by the Iraqis, he died three days later. Kuwait had become a nightmare for the sick or injured.

As Sara was leaving the city, she saw dead animals from the zoo laying by the roadside.

The Iraqis had released all the animals within the first few days of the occupation. They had used some for target practice but many had escaped to die slowly of starvation in the city. Some of Sara's friends tried to feed a starving zebra but their food supply was running low. After a few days they couldn't bear to hear the hungry bleating of the poor beast so they got up their nerve and shot it. There was a weakened and hungry elephant wandering the streets of Kuwait City. Used to the loving attention of its trainer, the elephant walked up to people and tried to get their attention by waving its trunk.

Starving animals, soldiers firing on children, friends dying from lack of simple medical care—this was the worst kind of nightmare. Now living in London, Sara is living proof of how far the long arm of Saddam Hussein stretches, keeping Kuwaitis on constant alert.

◆
Haya Hakima

Haya was sleeping soundly on the morning of August 2, when her younger sister ran into her bedroom yelling that their house was surrounded by Iraqi soldiers. Haya told her sister to stop playing stupid jokes and go back to sleep. She was in no mood for such gags. When her sister told her to get up and look for herself, Haya dragged herself out of bed. When she saw the armed men wearing Iraqi uniforms she staggered and lost her voice.

An established businesswoman, Haya was concerned abut her business and her employees. She tried to leave her house and drive to the business district, but the Iraqi soldiers told her there was a curfew and forced her to go back inside. The next three days were the longest of Haya's life. Finally, the curfew was lifted for daytime travel.

Haya found the business district totally destroyed. One of her Hungarian employees had been beaten by the Iraqis. Unluckily, the poor man had worn a beeper, and the Iraqis, unaware of its function, reacted to its beeping as though it were a bomb. They threw the man to the ground and beat him viciously. They carefully took the beeper, put it aside, and then ran away. When it didn't explode, they came back and beat the Hungarian some more. It was obvious to Haya that the Iraqi troops were nervous and had no clear orders on how to treat the civilians.

Haya was strong for six days, certain that the Iraqis would be forced to leave. On the seventh day, she realized that the occupation was not going to end quickly. Suddenly, the business she had worked hard for ten years to build was gone. Slowly the realization sunk in that it was going to be close to impossible to deal with the enemy.

When Haya visited her aunt's house, she was shocked to find her grandmother's Koran torn to tiny pieces and scattered all over the house. Portions of it were even in the toilet. Soldiers' boot marks were on top of it. Her grandmother's prayer mat was cut into pieces. This desecration of the Koran was intolerable, the action of beasts.

Shortly afterwards, seven Iraqi soldiers raped two young girls, ages 18 and 19, in front of their parents in an area close by. Haya's parents decided it was time to leave Kuwait. Packed and ready to depart, the family was told of disturbing developments on the border. Friends and neighbors were returning without their men. The Iraqi soldiers were stopping the Kuwaitis at the border and asking the men to step outside the cars. All men between the ages of 17 and 45 were taken aside, rounded up, loaded onto trucks, and driven away. The women, children, and older men were allowed to leave. Most Kuwaitis turned back in hopes that they could trace their men. Since Haya had a 22-year-old brother, her parents could not think of leaving Kuwait. They could not risk having their son be taken prisoner or quite possibly murdered. At this point, they could put nothing past the Iraqis. It was decided that Haya and her sister should leave.

Knowing full well that they might never see their family again, Haya and her sister said good-bye. The two sisters took a final drive through Kuwait and said farewell to their country. It was not the same city they had known.

At the border, Haya thanked God that her parents and brother had stayed behind. She saw Iraqi soldiers surround the vehicles and grab all the young men from inside. She saw boys as young as 14 taken from screaming parents. When, because the Kuwaitis had been alerted of the dangers, no men above the age of 17 were arriving at the borders, the Iraqis simply lowered the age requirement. Haya said that the boys were hanging on to their parents and the parents were hanging on to their sons and the Iraqis were beating everyone. She saw young boys thrown like so much meat into trucks. Their parents wailed as they were driven away. Would they ever be seen again?

Haya saw one old man at the border. He was at least eighty-five years old, and the grief he felt at leaving Kuwait was evident. He was staring back at Kuwait while tears rolled down his cheeks. Haya watched him, realizing that the agony of a nation was depicted in his face.

The Al-Sabahs

Salman Al-Sabah, Kuwait's ex-minister of justice, was unnerved from the very beginning by the massing of Saddam Hussein's troops. On Saturday, July 28, four days before the invasion, he expressed his suspicion that Hussein had plans to use his 100,000 troops. It was analogous, he felt, to having a loaded pistol held to your head with the assurance that it won't be fired. Why hold it there in the first place? Salman just didn't feel good about Hussein's actions.

The bad feeling stayed with him that entire week. On Wednesday night he drove with a group to the airport to meet the Crown Prince, who was returning to Kuwait City after the ill-fated meeting in Jeddah, Saudi Arabia. The Crown Prince told them that the meeting had not gone well and that the Iraqis had walked out of the meeting. Salman returned home with a strong feeling that the Iraqis would attack Kuwait that very night. He went to bed troubled. To Salman Al-Sabah, history has proven that the Kuwaitis are a peace-loving and generous people. They helped Saddam Hussein when he needed their help and then got hit in the back for doing so.

Sheik Badar Mohammed Al-Sabah

Sheik Badar Mohammed Al-Sabah, an ex-ambassador to the Gulf area, was in a coma in a Boston hospital when the Iraqis overtook Kuwait. He had undergone a kidney transplant, after which he remained in a coma for two weeks.

His family hovered by his bedside and prayed for his recovery. They were happy but stunned when Badar came out of the coma, for his first words were, "Did Iraq invade Kuwait?" He had been unconscious when the event occurred and his family had dreaded telling him the awful news. The only explanation that could be given was that Badar was able to hear the television even though he was in a coma.

An indulgent father with a gentle manner, Badar worried about the effect of the invasion on his children. He has tried to look at the incident from all angles and come up with a reason for such an unreasonable situation. It is an impossible task.

"Don Padro" Al-Sabah

Don Padro[*] knows everything about Saddam Hussein: the moment of his birth on April 28, 1937; his life as a peasant boy who grew up to be a crude and uneducated man; the first time he killed a man, before the age of 20; his manner of handling disagreements—not with dialogue but with a gun. Don Padro is a civilized man, and Saddam Hussein makes him feel uncivilized. He is ready to shoot the dictator on the spot, but has no way getting to him. Certainly, if Don Padro has his way, a large part of the world's problems will be erased in a flash.

Dr. Souad Abdullah Al-Sabah

Souad Al-Sabah, a renowned Arab poet and writer, cannot forget the gigantic efforts made by all the people of Kuwait as they supported Iraq during its long war with Iran. Everyone worked diligently in his own way to promote the cause of Iraq. The Kuwaiti government provided Saddam with financial support and unlimited political backing. Kuwaiti people contributed morally and materially to the Iraqi war effort.

---

[*]"Don Padro" is a code name.

As a writer and poet, Souad applied all of her skills, imagination, and feelings in support of Iraq. She was there with her pen and her voice to express herself loudly and clearly in articles, poems, and speeches. On numerous occasions she was subjected to criticism due to her unlimited support of Iraq.

So it was with utter disbelief that Souad reacted to Saddam Hussein's invasion of Kuwait. She was sickened by the extent and the magnitude of the atrocities that accompanied the invasion and felt personally betrayed, hurt, and deceived.

Before the invasion, Souad spent a large portion of her day, as a wife and mother, with family responsibilities. She devoted at least half a day per week in receiving many Kuwaiti women in accordance with Kuwaiti tradition. (These sessions are called diwaniyahs. Men meet with men, women, and young adults with their friends to discuss matters of interest including politics, regional events, family, and country matters. Many Kuwaitis say that these gatherings have insured the close relationship that exists between all Kuwaitis.) What was left of Souad's time was devoted primarily to research and writing. She regularly covered topical economic and political issues to a number of Kuwaiti and Arab newspapers. Souad was always at work on one or two books on economics and/or poetry and Arabic literature.

Once the unthinkable was accepted, the Kuwaitis banded together, using the same energy to assist each other as they once had to help their country's invader. Every Kuwaiti worked around the clock to support their fellow desperate citizens, and help each other overcome their problems. In the days following August 2, scores of Kuwaitis were escaping without money, food, clothes, or the ability to find a home. Teams and committees were formed, each person contributing according to their area of expertise. There was no seniority or superiority in the committees. Everyone worked to reclaim the land and the life they had lost. Since the invasion, Souad has produced a flood of articles and poems condemning his action. This translation appeared in the daily Alsharg Al Awsat on August 14, 1990.

We Shall Keep Standing*

We shall keep standing
Like all lofty trees,
We shall remain furious

---

*Printed by permission of Souad Al-Sabah

Like the waves of the Sea of Kuwait,
You will never steal daylight from us,
You who arrived at dawn on a tank,
Have you ever seen a tank
making dialogue?
Never will you find in my homeland
A single star to guide you,
A single palm tree to remember you,
A single child to thank you,
You may have damaged our doors,
You may have terrified our children,
You may have ruined the Kuwaiti house,
But we will nevertheless remain
Just as trees do,
Just as rivers, jungles, valleys, and stars do
So remove your knives from our flesh,
Return to us our pearls and shells,
And return from whence you came
For we adults and children
oppose oppression
Wherever you walk on Kuwaiti soil
You will feel the sand turning into stones
And the sea becoming fire,
You who used to be a neighbor
You who terrified scores of gazelle
Removing kohl from eyes
is not any victory
What you call the great epic

Is suicide in my terms
You neighbor who ruined my house
Though I built a home for him
deep in my heart,
I do feel broken, oppressed, amazed
My dreams are kicked away
by frustration,
You who gave me desert
in exchange for water,
Blockage in exchange for horizon,
Occupation in exchange for support,
Don't blame me for becoming crazed.
You have left no option for anyone,
You who trod on our bodies
at dawn's break,
What have we done?
Have we ever broken love terms?
We have been with you in good days,
We have been with you in bad days.
Why are you planting your sword
in my waist?
Why are you molesting my family?
What is the use of screams
When I am crushed to the bone?
Who can hear my voice
When I am buried under the debris,
When an Arab sword stabs me in the back?
History becomes a shame,

When my cousin slaughters me in bed,
The Pan-Arab dream becomes as dust.

(Arab women wear kohl eyeliner to enhance
the beauty of their eyes. The reference above
suggests that taking the beauty of the eye is not
a victory because the eye remains.)

Aware of the issues that will face her people
upon their return to Kuwait, Souad has no
doubt that the Kuwaitis will return. The only
question is when. Then the people of Kuwait
will have to address themselves to the lessons
learned from their bitter experience. There will
be deep emotional scars and physical injuries.
The magnitude of the task which awaits them
will be tremendous. The invasion of Kuwait
shook the very foundation of the whole population. The country suffered considerable damage and destruction. Despite its complete
isolation, the early reports that leaked out con-
firmed a very bleak picture of systematic
destruction of the country's infrastructure.

Souad's personal experiences has made her
think a great deal about the status of refugees.
Always in history, the term refugee had been
equated with that of someone who is living.
Now Saddam Hussein has created a new kind
of refugee, a dead refugee.

Souad's uncle was one of the first dead refugees. Upon hearing about the invasion, he suffered a stroke and later died in a London hospital. He had one simple wish for his family: to bury him in Kuwait. Souad and her family agonized for days over his request, finally recognizing that they were unable to fulfill his last wish. They found that the search for a grave is not an easy matter when you are out of your own land. But one fact was proven: the people of Britain, to whom her family had no blood ties, and who have been regarded by many Arabs as enemies, were more merciful to the refugee body of her uncle than was Saddam Hussein.

Sheikher Fadila Al-Aazbi Al-Sabah

The widow of Fahd Ahmed Al-Sabah, Fadila heard about the death of her husband in the worse kind of way: over British television.

She had just spoken with Fahd the day before, on August 1, and had hung up the phone with the usual goodbyes. It was to be Fadila's last conversation with her husband.

Fadila had left Kuwait in July so that she could take her youngest son, Dari, who was 19, to a hospital in the States for treatment of a special ear problem. She had taken their one daughter, Bebi, who was 15, along with her. After Dari's medical treatment was completed, Fadila had travelled with the children to London. There they planned to meet the rest of the family and take the summer holiday together. Fahd and their three eldest sons were scheduled to join Fadila, Dari, and Bebi in London on August 2. But the invasion of Kuwait had changed everything.

From the moment that Fadila heard the news about the invasion, she sat in front of the television, stunned and afraid for the people of Kuwait. She never felt her husband was in danger. Fahd was a strong and tough man, a hero to those that knew him, and he knew how to take care of himself. And, she had little fear for her sons for she had no doubt that Fahd would protect them from any harm.

Fadila was sitting alone and listening to the television news hour when the announcer reported that Sheik Fahd Al-Sabah, the Emir's younger brother, had been killed while defending Dasman Palace, the Emir's home. Too shocked to move, she sat listening but not hearing the remainder of the news. When her sisters and friends heard the report, they all rushed to her side.

Fadila managed to tell her son Dari of his father's death, but hesitated to break the news to her youngest, Bebi. She felt her daughter was so close to her father she might not be able to stand the shock of knowing he was dead. Instead, she told her daughter that her father had been wounded very badly but was going to be all right.

News was scanty as to the exact details of Fahd's death and Fadila began to worry about the safety of her sons. Where were they? Had they been with their father when he was killed? Did they know their father was dead? What was happening inside Kuwait? Pacing the floor, she waited to hear from her sons.

Finally Fadila received two separate phone calls, neither of which brought her the news for which she was hoping.

Talal, her 25-year-old son, called to say that he and his brothers were alive but that he had been shot in his left leg and left arm.

That was the last Fadila had heard from her sons. She had no way of knowing if Tala had received medical attention or what had happened in the following days during the deadly clashes between Kuwaiti resistance and the Iraqis.

The second phone call was even more of a shock. Fadila knew that it was a long distance call. Hoping it would be good news about her children, she was dumbfounded to hear the operator say that Iraq was calling, and startled to hear crying and shouting on the phone. Then she recognized the voice of one of her Filipino maids that had taken care of her grandchildren in Kuwait. The girl was on the verge of a breakdown. Between sobs, she gave Fadila details on what had really happened in Fadila's home the morning of the invasion.

When Sheik Fahd heard of the invasion, he jumped in his car and drove to the Emir's palace. He did not awaken his sons. While driving to the palace, he saw that the Iraqis were swarming all over the city. He became concerned that his sons might go out and get involved in the battle. He called the Indian houseservant from the car phone and told him not to let the boys leave the house. He gave instructions that they were to stay at the house and that he would soon return. The servant told him that he was too late. The three boys had already heard about the attack, dressed in their military uniforms, and had left the house with their weapons. That phone call was the last known communication with Fahd.

The servants were alone in the house when the Iraqis came. There was a large group of soldiers and they were abusive to Fadila's employees. The soldiers pushed and shoved them and held guns in their faces. They started looting the house of all the valuables an told the servants they were going to burn it down. The soldiers said that they had been told to destroy all property belonging to members of the Al-Sabah family. There were four Filipino girls working in the house in their early twenties and two in their forties. There was also an Indian family which included children plus a few other Indian employees. The Iraqi soldiers grabbed the two young and pretty Filipinos and began to rip off their clothes in front of everyone. In terror, the two older Filipinos and the others fled. They heard the screams of the two young girls as they left the area. In a short while, frantic with worry about their friends, the older Filipinos slipped back to the house and peeped inside the windows. There were about 15 soldiers taking turns raping the two young Filipinos. Unable to help their friends, the two fled once again. They watched from a distance as the soldiers left. But, the house was destroyed in moments by explosives. The girls said the walls were only a foot high. They did not see the two younger Filipinos come out. Fadila's home was totally destroyed.

Within days after the Iraqi invasion, Fadila learned that her husband was dead, one of her sons shot, the whereabouts of two other sons unknown, her home destroyed, some of her employees raped and quite possibly dead, and her country invaded and occupied by a cruel enemy.

Sheik Fahd Ahmed Al-Jabir Al-Sabah

Sheik Fahd Al-Sabah could have fled the invading army, but the thought never entered his mind. Instead, he ran toward the Iraqis. He was killed the first day of the invasion by Iraqi soldiers while he was defending the Dasman Palace, the home of his brother, the Emir of Kuwait.

Fahd had an aura that drew others to him. He struck a cord in people and they responded to his magnetism. He had a special interest in the youth of Kuwait and took special pains to listen to their simplest problems. He was a caring and devoted father to his children. Everyone who met Fahd came away feeling they had met an exceptional man. He was a brave man, the kind of man who was willing to die for his beliefs.

As time passed and the special traits of Fahd were known, I realized that he would not have sought out nor wanted special recognition for his bravery during the invasion of his country. Instead, he would have agonized over each life lost, insisting that they, and not he, be recognized.

His Highness Sheik Saud Al-Abdullah Al-Salem Al-Sabah, Crown Prince and Prime Minister

The Crown Prince of Kuwait arrived at the Kuwaiti airport on the night of August 1, 1990, exhausted from a trip to Saudi Arabia. He had spent the previous few days in Jedda, meeting with "Voices of Saddam Hussein" (high officials of the Iraqi government that spout verbatim the dictator). There, under the auspices of Saudi Arabia's King Fahd, he tried to come to a rational agreement with irrational people. The Iraqis walked out of the meeting with the problem unresolved. The Crown Prince returned to Kuwait. But he arrived without fear of an attack for the Saudi King had asked for and received assurances that Saddam Hussein's armies would not march on Kuwait.

The Crown Prince went straight to the home of his cousin, the Emir, where he reported the result of the meeting in Saudi Arabia. Afterward, he went home and went to bed. At around 1:30 A.M. the next morning, August 2, he was awakened by the Minister of Defense with the unexpected news that Saddam's armies were inside Kuwait's borders. Dressing quickly, he accompanied the Minister of Defense to the Operations Room to see if they could gauge the seriousness of the attack. Was it a grab for the Bubiyan oilfields and the Warba islands or was Hussein coming in for the whole country? It soon became evident that Iraq's armies were not going to stop at the Bubiyan oilfield or go for the islands. All reports had the enemy army advancing toward the city at a rapid pace. The Crown Prince was first shocked and angry at the Iraqi deception. Without doubt, they walked from the meeting in Jedda as a pretense for the attack. The officials had probably known all along of Hussein's plan for a dawn attack on Kuwait. The meeting had been a decoy for the Iraqi duplicity.

By 5:30 A.M. the Operations Room was crammed with Kuwaiti ministers and high officials. The Crown Prince told his colleagues that they were in an unsafe place and due to the seriousness of the attack, they would have to move their base. The Iraqi soldiers were advancing much more rapidly than anyone could have imagined. The ministers scattered in different directions in the city and the Crown Prince and his driver left together and drove away from the city. For some inexplicable reason, a sudden inner feeling that harm would come to the Emir caused the Crown Prince to instruct his driver to change the route. He picked up the car phone and dialed the Emir's home. He told him "I am coming to take you away." Then he told the driver to drive very fast to His Highness. When he arrived at the Emir's home, they had a quick discussion of what to do and where to go. They would decide on a place and then realize it would not be safe from the Iraqis. The Crown Prince would name a location and the Emir would disagree; the Emir would name one spot and the Crown Prince would disagree. By this time the Iraqis were advancing into the city. The rulers of Kuwait knew with sinking hearts that there were very few safe places. Although neither wanted to leave, they knew that the legitimate government had to survive, even if the country were taken. Finally, they decided to drive to the Kuwaiti Police Post, which is close to the border of Saudi Arabia. It was a compromise of sorts. They would still be in their country but close to Saudi Arabia in the event the

Iraqis effected a complete takeover of Kuwait. And so they quickly made their way across the land. Fortunately, The Crown Prince followed his instincts; shortly after their departure, the Iraqis targeted and completely destroyed the Emir's palace.

The first thing the Emir and the Crown Prince did when they arrived at the Police Post was to call King Fahd of Saudi Arabia. Fearful for their safety, the King insisted that they come to Saudi Arabia. King Fahd's revered father, Abdul Aziz Al-Saud, had lived in exile in Kuwait from 1894 until the retaking of Saudi Arabia in 1902. The ancestor of the current Kuwaiti rulers, Mubarek Al-Sabah, had welcomed the exiled Saudis and assisted them in their successful bid to reclaim the desert kingdom. Evidently, King Fahd did not forget that his family was in similar circumstances in the last days of the 19th century. The Crown Prince agreed with King Fahd that the Emir should go but he wanted to stay as long as possible.

By 5:00 P.M. the Crown Prince received news that the Iraqis were headed toward the Border Post and were amassing their troops right before him. King Fahd, following the action of the Iraqi troops from across the border, called the Crown Prince insisting that he leave the area and go to Damman (in Saudi Arabia). The Crown Prince refused. It was not until the Emir, who was with King Fahd, got on the phone and ordered him to leave that the Crown Prince reluctantly drove to Damman. Bent and determined to remain in Kuwait, however, he stayed only four hours and then returned to the Border Post. There he stayed until the following afternoon. When he saw the numerous tanks massing and the number of soldiers increasing, he felt sure that the Iraqi troops were planning to invade Saudi Arabia. He and a trusted aide stood and counted the tanks. Finally the Crown Prince gave in to the huge force before him and went back to Damman.

The Crown Prince took his anger and put it to good work. He spoke with the Emir and they agreed that the Crown Prince would fly to Egypt to meet with President Mubarak and set up an Arab Summit in order to try to get the Iraqis out of Kuwait.

The Crown Prince fully understood the multitude of problems that faced the Kuwaiti people and was proud of the high morale of the people after a catastrophe that left families separated, and many people dead and injured. His first goal was to work within the world community to get Kuwait back. Secondly, he anticipated the return to Kuwait and began to draw up plans to repair the damage done by the marauding soldiers of Saddam Hussein.

Sheik Jaber Al-Ahmad Al-Sabah, The Emir of Kuwait

The present ruler of Kuwait was born in 1928, the third son of the late Sheik Ahmad Al-Jaber Al-Sabah, the former ruler of Kuwait.

In 1928, Kuwait was a very different place than it is in 1990. The young Jaber grew up in a mud palace and lived a quiet and modest life. His family had handled the financial and political affairs of Kuwait since 1752; therefore, he was raised with an awareness of regional politics. He had heard the elders discuss the rule of the Ottomans and the influence of the European powers. The Al-Sabahs became adept at bargaining with the superpowers for the best deal for tiny Kuwait. Jaber learned early that a country as small as Kuwait had to learn the art of negotiation in order to survive. But life was not totally serious. Jaber had plenty of playmates who remember him as being a fair-minded and likeable youth.

Jaber's elementary education was received in Kuwait in the Al-Mubarakiya and Al-Ahmadiah schools. Private tutors completed his education in Arabic literature, English, basic science, and religion.

In 1938, when Jaber was only ten years old, oil was discovered in Kuwait. There was no way of knowing the impact this discovery would have on the country or his life. Little could he know that he would grow up to lead one of the richest nations on earth.

Due to the war in Europe, the impact of the oil was delayed. It was not until 1946 that the oil taps were turned on and exports started. Even so, the price of oil was kept artificially low by the Western oil companies who managed to keep the bulk of the profits for themselves. It was not until the sixties that oil revenues began to change the way most people lived.

At age 21 Jaber started his public service career as director of public security. At age 31 he was made the first minister of finance. Six years later, in 1965, he was appointed prime minister and one year later, Crown Prince. He was proclaimed Emir on December 31, 1977.

Since that time he has won the respect and support of an overwhelming majority of Kuwaitis. Surprisingly unpretentious considering his vast wealth, the Emir earned the reputation of a man who enjoyed the simple things in life. He had grown up without the trappings of wealth and somehow he never embraced the extravagant lifestyle so common with "new money." Unlike most Arab rulers, he disliked travel and spend the bulk of his time in Kuwait.

The Emir is best known for his quality of fair-mindedness. On December 12, 1983, Kuwait was targeted and hit in six locations (including the U.S. Embassy, where four were left dead and 20 were wounded) by the Iranian-backed terrorist group call the Al-Dawa (meaning, "the call"). Dead and wounded Kuwaitis were left in the rubble. The leader of the group and 16 others were soon captured, brought to trial, and sentenced to death. At the time of the 1990 invasion, the 17 terrorists were still imprisoned in Kuwait. Time and again, the Emir had been presented with the paperwork to execute the 17, but he thought that the young men had been brainwashed by the Iranian regime and wondered if they might be rehabilitated.

When the Iraqi president attacked Iran, the Emir provided him financial and political support. The Iranians had menaced Kuwait since the overthrow the the Shah and the real enemy, Saddam, cloaked his intentions with a shrewd propaganda ploy. He courted the Kuwaitis and won their trust. Thus, the attack from Saddam was unexpected and caught the Emir and the Kuwaitis off guard.

When word came that the Iraqis had crossed the border, the Emir was determined not to leave his country. Only the insistence of the Crown Prince and King Fahd of Saudi Arabia convinced him of the necessity of saving the legitimate government.

A slim figure with fair skin and coal black eyes, the ruler of the Kuwaitis is quiet to the point of being shy. Content out of the limelight, the Emir stays as close as possible to Kuwait at the official Kuwaiti government-in-exile quarters at the Sheraton Hotel in the hills of Taif, Saudi Arabia. From there he coordinates the numerous diplomatic, financial, and resistance efforts that are necessary to wrest his land and citizens from the Iraqi grip.

Alarmed by the growing abuses of the Iraqis against his trapped citizens in Kuwait, the Emir travelled to the United States and addressed the United Nations General Assembly in New York on September 27, 1990. Portions of this speech painfully highlight the scourge of the Iraqi invasion.[*]

---

*Reprinted with permission of the Kuwaiti government.

I speak from this rostrum today as my peaceful country is passing through extremely harsh circumstances that have given rise to an unprecedented crisis in the history of the United Nations, which, since its inception, has sought to uphold justice on the basis of international law. Indeed, the Security Council has demonstrated that role by recently adopting a series of firm resolutions in the face of naked and brutal aggression against the State of Kuwait.

Today, I bring to you the message of a peace-loving nation. A nation that had consistently worked for peace; a nation that reached out with a helping hand to all those who truly needed help; a nation that sought mediation and reconciliation among adversaries. It is this very nation whose security and stability have been trampled upon as a result of its abiding belief in lofty principles inspired by our true Moslem faith and echoed in universal charters, pacts, and codes of morality.

Today, I plead before you the cause of a people whose land, until so recently, was a beacon for peaceful coexistence and genuine brotherhood among the family of nations. A people whose national territory was a gathering place for individuals from various peaceful nations who sought a decent and dignified life through constructive work. Some of these people have been made homeless, wanderers living only on hope in their banishment, while others have become prisoners or fighters, refusing, even at the risk of their own lives, to surrender or yield to occupation with all its violence and brutality.

The crisis of Kuwait is a manifold tragedy, whose dire consequences affect not only Kuwaitis but other peoples as well. In fact, it has jeopardized stability in the world, especially in the Gulf region.

I came here to tell you of the horrors and suffering we are enduring both inside and outside our occupied homeland, and to put before you our just case. Expecting you to act in good conscience, we are confident that the only measure that will win your endorsement is support for our legitimate right to liberate our land. Furthermore, we trust that you will not waver in deciding on the measures needed to compel the invading aggressors to restore the legitimate authority and to put an end to the barbaric acts and deviations.

The aggression by the Iraqi regime against the State of Kuwait which resulted in occupation and the Iraqis' vicious attempts to annex Kuwait in flagrant violation of all charters, norms of conduct, and treaties, including those legal instruments concluded between the two countries and deposited right here with the United Nations, is not an ordinary conflict between two states over a piece of land. Rather, the Iraqi aggression was the culmination of a premeditated scheme to occupy and seize the entire state by force of arms.

This Iraqi regime has invented false pretexts and untenable claims against my peaceful and peace-loving country. Iraq was bent on sweeping through the entire territory of Kuwait, violating its sovereignty and violating the sanctity of Kuwaiti citizens' lives and property. As a consequence, rape, destruction, terror, and torture are now the rule of the day in the once peaceful and tranquil land of Kuwait. Hundreds of thousands of Kuwaiti citizens along with nationals of various other countries who were our guests have been made homeless and many of them have had their life savings robbed. Hundreds have lost their lives. Others have been held hostage. Indeed, at this very moment, an intense campaign of terror, torture, and humiliation continues unabated in that dear land. We receive daily reports of massacres and continuing systematic armed looting and destruction of state assets and individual property.

Against all these odds, an enormous source of solace to us has been the position taken by virtually all countries of the world in support of Kuwait's rights.

In closing, may I take this opportunity, Mr. President, to address a few words to my people, my kinfolk, the loyal sons and daughters of Kuwait, from this august forum, a forum for justice and fairness, a forum for guidance and hope, to assure each and every one of you that Allah, the Almighty, will ultimately secure triumph for us, thanks to your struggle and resolve, thanks to the gracious role of the United Nations, thanks to the support lent to us by our brethren and friends along with all people of good conscience throughout the world. The withdrawal of the invaders is, God willing, undoubtedly imminent. We shall return to our Kuwait, the oasis of safety and peace, which embraces all Kuwaitis and foreigners living in our midst as brothers. Together, we will join hands in concert and harmony to secure our development and progress. This will be a fulfillment of God's promise as rendered in the following verse:

Oh ye who believe,
If you will aid Allah,
He will aid you,
And plant your feet firmly.

And, whose word can be truer than Allah's? Thank you and may Allah, our Lord, bring you all peace and grace.

Epilogue

Like a weed whose shade is poison,
Overgrows this region's foison,
Sheaves of whom are ripe to come,
To destruction's harvest-home,
Men must reap the things they sow,
Force from force must ever flow,
Or worse; but 'tis a better woe
That love or reason cannot change
The despot's rage, the slave's revenge
                —Percy Bysshe Shelley

After centuries of living in abject poverty, the people of Kuwait found hope for the future with the discovery of oil. Unlike most people who are presented with unearned and instant wealth, the Kuwaitis wisely invested their money and worked hard to form an infrastructure that was impressive to even the most advanced Western countries. Unfortunately, this realized goal of "the good life" brought about resentment from other peoples in the region who found themselves less favored by geological fate.

While it is true that there is great disparity between the "haves" and "have-nots" of the Middle East, it is also true that the oil-rich countries have a record of giving generously to their less-prosperous Arab brothers. The Kuwaitis and the Saudis have been particularly charitable in this regard.

Until Saddam Hussein's invasion, the Kuwaitis were unaware that their generosity had failed to win the respect and affection of their neighbors. In fact, the Kuwaitis' efforts produced the opposite effect. Wounded pride grew into jealousy and malice.

As I traveled through the Middle East during the days immediately following the invasion, I spoke with many Arabs from the lands of "have-nots." I was surprised by the comments made and the spite with which they were spoken:

> Syrian: "They got what they deserved. They were arrogant."
>
> Palestinian: "I'm with Saddam! Those people needed to feel the sand up their noses!"
>
> Lebanese: "Good! I want those bastards to know what war feels like."

Lebanese: "They had too much. Let
them eat dates!"

Over and over, I listened as the very people
who had benefited the most from Kuwaiti generosity rejoiced at the fall of Kuwait. And yet,
some of these people might actually go hungry
without the flow of money from their wealthy
kin.

Shocked by these reactions and curious to
know their cause, I asked these men and
women for explanations, but the responses I
received were unsatisfactory. There was much
groping for an adequate defense of their position, and when none could be found, I bore the
brunt of their indignation. They told me I could
never understand because I was not Arab.
These comments came from some of the very
people who, years before, had told me I was
more Arab than they. The illogic of their position and their focused hatred not only disappointed me, but also caused me great sadness.
Oil and economics wrap all the countries of the
world within the violence of the Middle East
and such attitudes do not bode well for future
stability within the region.

At the time of this writing, Kuwait is still
occupied by Iraq. Saddam Hussein has
repeated his oath that he will never give up

Kuwait, the nineteenth province of Iraq. President George Bush has proclaimed that Saddam Hussein's occupation of Kuwait "will not stand," and that the dictator will leave Kuwait voluntarily or by force. The UN has passed its twelfth resolution to the Persian Gulf crisis; Security Council Resolution 678 gives Iraq until January 15, 1991, to withdraw from Kuwait or face possible military action by UN member states. The rulers of Kuwait have assured their people that "the Kuwaiti government will not spare any resources, no matter how much, in order to liberate our beloved country." The Kuwaiti people are gathering in the sands of Saudi Arabia and have vowed to fight to the last man to regain their homeland. The U.S. Navy reports that the blockade of Iraq is nearly 100% effective. The escalation of pressure continues to build and the world is bracing for yet another killing field in the sands of the Middle East.

What will happen? How will this tangled web of declarations be resolved? Will Saddam Hussein yield and leave Kuwait, or will thousands of young men on all sides pay with their lives for the greed and folly of a dictator? No one can say for certain, including George Bush and Saddam Hussein, for the actions of one depend upon the actions and reactions of the other. However, it does seem most likely that the country of Kuwait will eventually be restored to its rightful owners, whether by war or negotiation.

Restored Kuwait will not be the country its citizens fled. Kuwait will be devastated. Every Kuwaiti to whom I spoke told me that they only wanted the land beneath their feet, and to a large degree that is just what they will be getting. A war to dislodge the Iraqi army will destroy the country, as will an undefeated but humiliated retreating army. The outcome will be the same for the Kuwaiti homeland.

Once Kuwait is liberated, the enormous task of rebuilding will have to begin immediately. How the Kuwaitis go about this task will determine the futures of their children and grandchildren. The physical reconstruction will take years to complete and will require all the revenues from both their investments and their oil.

The psychological recovery of the people will be slower still. The strength of resolve of every Kuwaiti citizen will be tested again and again. The decisions they make about their economic, military, political, and social future will be crucial to their long-term survival as a nation.

The Kuwaiti government in exile is determined to make the return to Kuwait as orderly as possible. They have not been sitting idly by waiting for the restoration of their country. Within days of Iraq's invasion, committees were formed to plan and facilitate an orderly return. Teams of specialists have been organized and positioned in Bahrain, Saudi Arabia, and the United Arab Emirates, where they stand ready to speed into Kuwait as soon as the order is given.

Kuwaiti government and military officials will be the first to enter freed Kuwait. A type of National Guard will be stationed around the country to maintain order during the chaos that will surely follow Iraq's withdrawal.

Once order has been established and military threats such as Iraqi booby traps and minefields have been cleared, medical teams will begin to arrive to provide assistance to the sick and wounded. Since Iraq has emptied the Kuwaiti hospitals of equipment and supplies, the most severe medical cases will be evacuated into neighboring countries and others will receive treatment in Kuwaiti hospitals from special emergency units transported in with the medical teams. A special committee will assess the condition of the medical infrastructure and begin ordering the necessary supplies. Supply lines will begin to run from friendly neighboring countries and airlifts from Western allies will begin to bring in food and medical equipment.

The Kuwaiti government will request citizens presently living outside the country to refrain from entering Kuwait while order is being restored. This particular aspect will prove to be difficult. Kuwaitis by the thousands are pacing on the borders of their country waiting for the first possible moment to rush inside to check on loved ones. Considering the length of the Saudi border and the Kuwaiti shoreline, pandemonium is a certainty. It is doubtful that returning refugees will think to carry in their own supply of foodstuffs, so hunger may be a problem in the early days of the return. The military presence now located in Saudi Arabia may be called upon to assist the Kuwaiti civilians.

Teams of engineers and technicians will attempt to reconstruct the electricity and telephone services. The weather is relatively mild from January through March so hopefully work on cooling systems can be delayed while other, more major, problems are given priority.

As soon as the electricity, telephone, food, and medical problems are resolved, the government will authorize the return of all Kuwaiti citizens. Joy and celebration will rule the land for a few days while families are reunited.

As the Kuwaitis pause and take stock of their losses, anger and depression are to be expected. Teams of physicians and assistants will be on hand to help the people through the difficult moments of realization of just what they have lost. Many families will learn of the deaths of sons, brothers, fathers, or husbands, since the Iraqis targeted and killed many of the Kuwaiti men.

Saddam Hussein has planted explosives in the Kuwaiti oilfields, so there is little doubt as to their fate. Be it through war or negotiation, most experts agree that whether Iraqi troops march or run out of Kuwait, they will systematically blow up the oil rigs. Even though oil-digging equipment is already in place in neighboring countries and oilfield firefighters are organized, years will pass before Kuwait returns to the same oil-producing capacity that existed prior to the August 2 invasion.

Luckily for the Kuwaitis, the government has saved and invested during its years of plenty. The General Reserve Fund and the Future Generations Reserves, along with other investments, will be used to rebuild.

Whereas all Kuwaitis I interviewed swore they would work without a salary for as long as necessary to rebuild their country, the government will find it essential to provide citizens with food, shelter, and medical care. A stipend for each individual will be set and basic needs will be met.

The former thriving banking system is now nonexistent. The vaults have been emptied and all records destroyed. Companies and private citizens will be asked to produce records of previous accounts. Efforts will be made to justify the wrongs committed, but in view of lost records, it will be difficult to reach equitable settlements in most cases. Quite simply, most savings are simply lost to private citizens and companies.

Considering the deliberate destructions by the invading army, it will take at least a year to structure guidelines for rebuilding the economic sector. It is estimated that within five years the economy will be judged healthy. By the year 2000, the Kuwaiti economy should be booming.

The Kuwaitis have a recurring nightmare. They dream that Saddam Hussein returns in five years after he has acquired nuclear weapons. He totally destroys Kuwait and leaves the country uninhabitable.

There is little doubt that all Kuwaitis want Saddam Hussein deposed. While they are not alone in this sentiment, they are the ones who will pay dearly if he retreats to Iraq with his armies intact.

Regardless of the outcome of Saddam Hussein, the government and the people of Kuwait recognize their vulnerability. Too small to defend themselves against a large and aggressive neighbor, too wealthy to inspire the sympathy of less-favored nations, they are making plans to avoid being the victims of future ambitious dictators.

In the past, the Kuwaitis refused a foreign military presence on their soil. While they now acknowledge their mistake, they still must consider the political environment in which they live and the animosities they would encounter if there is an American military base in Kuwait. The only possible alternatives to an American base would be to acquire nuclear weapons themselves, to welcome a UN military presence, or to form a multi-Arab army. Their decisions on this particular issue will have to be finalized once their country is restored and the condition of Saddam Hussein and his armies is analyzed. But, the feeling is that the Kuwaitis will opt for a multi-Arab army with a possible UN presence.

The only people who are calling for the overthrow of the Al-Sabah family are not of Kuwaiti nationality. While it is true that Saddam Hussein demands the exit of the Emir and the Crown Prince and that the Western media questions America's support of a monarchy, the people of Kuwait defend their government. I questioned every Kuwaiti I met about the future of a ruling family. Interestingly enough, not one Kuwaiti expressed a desire for the Emir or the Crown Prince to step down. Clearly, it was not fear of reprisal that prompted the Kuwaitis' support, but, instead, a genuine feeling of affection for their leaders. However, there was a general agreement that most Kuwaitis desire some change, such as a reinstatement of their lively parliament, more input in the affairs of government, and a reduction in the number of princes who benefit from the oil wealth. The majority of Kuwaitis expressed dismay that the outside world wanted to dictate their internal policies and felt sincerely that such decisions should be left to the Kuwaitis themselves.

When Saddam Hussein asked Kuwaitis to step forward and volunteer to head the new provisional government he established within days after the invasion, the world watched in amazement as not one Kuwaiti agreed to head the new government. Embarrassed and desperate, Saddam ushered in an Iraqi and declared he was a Kuwaiti. It is clear that the Kuwaitis want to remain with their leaders and their present government.

The Iraqi invasion threatened to remove all traces of Kuwaiti citizenship. By luck, during the month of November, a Kuwaiti managed to locate and slip computer discs containing the civil records of the citizens of Kuwait across the border into Saudi Arabia. These discs are now public record. They will ensure that the Kuwaitis will be able to reclaim their homes and businesses, now occupied by Iraqis who arrived in Kuwait by the thousands as soon as Saddam Hussein declared the country the nineteenth province of Iraq. Every person who lived in Kuwait as of August 1, 1990, whether Kuwaiti or of other nationalities, is listed on these discs. Should there be any difficulty in ascertaining just who is who, the authorities will ask neighbor to identify neighbor, and this identification process will travel chainlike across streets, neighborhoods, towns, cities, and countryside until all persons are verified as being who they say they are. By the time all Kuwaitis have returned, it is hoped that all imposters will have been deported. This process will be carried out within the neighborhoods of the expatriate community despite the probability that many of the Filipinos, Indians, Egyptians, and Palestinians who lived in this area and who fled Kuwait will never return.

Once the old neighborhoods have been reestablished, remaining social issues will be addressed. The schools and universities of Kuwait were gutted; it is thought that local neighborhood schools will substitute until such time as the public schools can be reopened. Since most Kuwaiti children have already missed one year of school, this will receive high priority.

Each individual will face the question of how to tackle the Iraqi/Palestinian question. I noted that the Kuwaitis who had lost everything, including members of their families, swore that Kuwait would no longer be a home for any Iraqi or Palestinian. Other Kuwaitis who had been out of the country at the time of the attack felt more forgiving toward Iraqi and Palestinian citizens. Since the Kuwaiti population swelled with these expatriate communities prior to the August 1990 attack, this issue will be debated for years to come.

The Kuwaitis are a deeply religious people and the mosques will serve as a haven. There Kuwaiti men, women, and children will receive the strength to resume their shattered lives. The close-knit family structure will bring needed fortitude to their resolve to pick up the pieces. All things considered, the Kuwaiti people face a formidable task, but, as they say, "Inshallah," or God willing, one day life will be good again.

This was a book about people and not about politics. But as in so many cases, politics were so closely intertwined with the realities of the story that they came together as one in the end. Politics shape our lives. Past years of self-serving policies in the Middle East region have come back to haunt us in 1990. One mistake has led to another and, as Saddam Hussein fed on those miscalculations, he grew to be a miscreant, set and ready to devour the lands and peoples around him. We are unsure as to the price we will pay to disarm and neutralize the monster of our making.

Many have already paid the price in Kuwait. Ahmed had his ear cut off and his eyes battered out of his head. He was then taken alive to his parents and executed while they were forced to watch.

Adil, who was a kind and caring social worker, was hideously tortured for days. His fingernails were ripped from his fingers. He was shocked and burned. He died screaming.

Dr. Abbas, a cancer specialist, refused to unhook cancer patients from lifesaving equipment and give the machines to Iraqi soldiers. He was shot in the head.

Ahmad, a husband and father, was forced to sit on burning metal. He died.

Sulaiman's head and face were forced into excrement. He choked to death. He was the only child of loving parents.

Mohammed was brutally beaten and dipped in hot oil. He died.

There are too many victims to name, too many sickening methods of death to imagine. And then there are the Kuwaitis who have been taken to Baghdad. To dwell on their fate is to feel unadulterated fear.

As we grapple with the dictator, Saddam Hussein, perhaps the lessons learned will stay in our memory and remind the people of the world to consider long-term prospects when making foreign-policy decisions.

One can only hope that the day will finally dawn when we will achieve the harmony and cooperation we envision.